Working with the Elephant

We've all been there. We are in a working group or at a meeting, discussing a topic or a challenge, and all the while, as a separate track running underneath our conversation, there is a subtext that no one explicitly addresses.

This is an example of 'the elephant in the room'. Most of us notice the elephant, it gets in the way, and it's difficult to deal with until someone points at it and says, 'There it is, let's take a look at it and reduce its impact.' With an engaging use of examples and questions, Lotte Svalgaard addresses how we can best deal with the elephant and thus promote job satisfaction, creativity and productivity. In the context of action, what we notice often recedes into the background and gradually slips out of focus until we eventually reconnect with our need to reflect and recreate a space for it. This book addresses the challenge of focusing on, holding on to and acting on what we notice 'in the middle of it all'. Maintaining a simultaneous focus on task and process – what we do and what we notice – is what the author defines as 'double awareness'. Double awareness is not only a core capacity but also a core challenge.

While the aim of *The Elephant in the Room* was to promote understanding and awareness of this core challenge and to inspire both reflection and action for anyone wishing to improve engagement in their workplaces, *Working with the Elephant* is taking this challenge a step further by providing ten core challenges in dealing with elephants in groups and organizations. It is a workbook about the difficult transition from avoidance to action. With help, support and tips, it guides readers to take action where it will make a difference for them, their group and the organization as a whole. It can be used as a workbook for *The Elephant in the Room* or it can be used independently.

Working with the Elephant

Methods for Engaging with the Unsaid in Groups and Organizations

Lotte Svalgaard

Routledge
Taylor & Francis Group
A PRODUCTIVITY PRESS BOOK

Designed cover image: Shutterstock
Illustrations created by Pernille Mühlbach.

First published 2025
by Routledge
605 Third Avenue, New York, NY 10158

and by Routledge
4 Park Square, Milton Park, Abingdon, Oxon, OX14 4RN

Routledge is an imprint of the Taylor & Francis Group, an informa business

Library of Congress Cataloging-in-Publication Data
Names: Svalgaard, Lotte, author.
Title: Working with the elephant : methods for engaging with the unsaid in groups and organizations / Lotte Svalgaard.
Description: Abingdon, Oxon ; New York, NY : Routledge, 2025. | Includes bibliographical references and index. |
Identifiers: LCCN 2024056588 (print) | LCCN 2024056589 (ebook) | ISBN 9781032950365 (hardback) | ISBN 9781032939476 (paperback) | ISBN 9781003582939 (ebook)
Subjects: LCSH: Communication in organizations. | Organizational behavior. | Organizational effectiveness. | Employee motivation. | Psychology, Industrial.
Classification: LCC HD30.3 .S9633 2025 (print) | LCC HD30.3 (ebook) | DDC 658.4/5--dc23/eng/20250221
LC record available at https://lccn.loc.gov/2024056588
LC ebook record available at https://lccn.loc.gov/2024056589

ISBN: 978-1-032-95036-5 (hbk)
ISBN: 978-1-032-93947-6 (pbk)
ISBN: 978-1-003-58293-9 (ebk)

DOI: 10.4324/9781003582939

Typeset in Garamond
by Deanta Global Publishing Services, Chennai, India

Contents

Preface

'What you do has to matter.'

(Alan Moore)

My 2023 book *The Elephant in the Room: Engaging with the Unsaid in Groups and Organizations* presents research and experiences from my many years of practice as an organizational psychologist. Since the release of the book, participants in elephant master classes, lectures and workshops have asked many good questions based on a deep-felt desire to get better at dealing with the big and small elephants in their workplace contexts: What do you when ...? And what if ...?

In *Working with the Elephant*, I discuss these questions and offer some answers.

The main reason why we want to be better at addressing the elephants in the room is that we want to engage, lead mindful lives, act on what we notice, be bolder and make a difference.

In an article in *Harvard Business Review*, Diane Coutu (2002) spoke with organizational psychologist and professor Edgar Schein to explore why it is that although 'everyone touts learning organizations [...] few actually exist'. In the interview, Schein offered the shocking and thought-provoking observation that, 'In the prison camps, 80% of the people survived the ordeal by being passive. That's generally the way it is in organizations.' Is that really true? Well, a fair amount of data from my own research and practice supports Schein's claim. So yes, it will take a major effort for us to find our voices in the contexts where they need to be heard for the sake of what matters to us, the groups we work in and our shared tasks. There are many reasons why we often remain passive when we ought to act on what we notice – and engage. It is not an easy task .

I have worked with many, both individuals and groups, who have curiously examined the personal and collective patterns and defensive routines that get in the way of their ability to act on what they notice and who have taken steps to establish new routines, driven by curiosity and the willingness to take interpersonal risks – because that is part of the job. The questions they ask reflect a desire for engagement and mindfulness, curiosity about how to proceed and hope of receiving a helping hand.

This workbook is underpinned by research and addresses some of the myriad curious and important questions that arise in our effort to build mindful cultures when we encounter, examine and curiously take elephants by the trunk.

Mindful living is a challenge. To many of us, however, it is also, increasingly, an obligation that we are keen to take on and take seriously.

Hence this workbook.

Welcome to *Working with the Elephant* – a guide to help you act on the insights in *The Elephant in the Room*. Based on ten challenges, the workbook addresses some of the issues I most commonly encounter and which many find to be the biggest obstacles for addressing and dealing with big and small elephant in the workplace. The challenges overlap, and some of them are interrelated. Focus on the areas that make most sense to you. The book suggests points that might be worth considering and provides ideas, support and tips to help you get started.

About the Author

Lotte Svalgaard holds PhD and MSc degrees in Business Psychology. Her research investigates how individuals can be awake and aware, show up and engage with challenges outside of their comfort zone. Her writing has appeared in Management Learning, Action Learning – Research and Practice, Socioanalysis and SAGE Research Method Cases. Her passion, to contribute to create more passionate and mindful organizations, makes up the platform for her work, her research and her authorships.

She is a global leadership development professional with extensive experience within group dynamics, experiential leadership development and organizational consultancy. Lotte is currently a senior leadership consultant and executive coach at INSEAD, consulting and coaching on senior executive leadership programs across multiple industries around the world.

Besides her work at INSEAD, she is a senior partner in Action Lab, where she designs and implements business-driven action learning programs for global companies. From 2001–2023, she was an associated professor, lecturer and supervisor at the Master of Psychology in Organisations at Roskilde University, Denmark. She is the author of *The Elephant in the Room: Engaging with the Unsaid in Groups and Organizations*, Routledge, 2023.

Introduction

From Avoidance to Action

In my research, I am interested in and curious about those situations that clearly call for action or for someone to speak up, but in which everyone instead remains silent and passive. This can occur in leadership or working groups with obvious conflicts or disagreements that go unaddressed, leading to situations that call for questions and curiosity.

> One of the questions I typically ask in these situations is,
>
> **Why don't they see it? Why aren't they noticing that he does not agree, that she is furious, that he is disengaged and so forth?**

I call this phenomenon *mindful avoidance*. The point is that it is not that we do not notice what is going on; we see it – and we avoid it. Even if we fleetingly connect with, and deep down, *know* that speaking up or taking action *would* be more helpful for ourselves, our group, and the task we are solving together.

Mindful action is the opposite: It involves speaking up and acting on what we notice and what is important to ourselves, the group we are part of, and/or our joint task. Approaching our own patterns with curiosity in an effort to understand them better can also help us understand what stops us from acting and what can help us to move from avoidance to action.

The consequences of mindful avoidance are significant. Mindful avoidance generates routines and habits – and, thus, cultures – of ignoring what we notice rather than engaging with the world around us and approaching it with curiosity. We become co-creators of avoidance cultures that are destructive to ourselves and to the work we do together. When we ignore what we notice – with the immediate purpose of self-protection – we miss out on engagement, learning and innovation.

All the questions that are incorporated into the ten challenges in this book revolve around the difficult transition from avoidance to action.

A Demand for Tools

How-questions often imply a demand for tools. Supportive tools that can assure us we are on the right path as we seek to *do* something else, something more, something new.

Tools are helpful, provided they are applied with mindfulness, increased awareness and reflection – and provided we use them wisely and avoid falling into the trap that learning researcher Peter Senge describes as the 'what we need here is a bigger hammer' syndrome (1990). With this comment, he was referring to the risk of overusing the tools we are familiar with – and comfortable using – even in situations that call for something other than what we have in our existing toolbox. When that happens, our familiar tools may, at worst, act as a defence against and a simplification of the complex work we encounter.

Whether a tool is effective or not depends on the situation, the character of our relationships and how we engage with the situation (and what we are bringing with us). Hence, the answer to the question 'Would this work in this case?' often begins with 'Well, that depends ...'

Tools easily become obsolete in a world that has moved from complicated to complex, since this change means that,

> Even though there are identifiable patterns, they do not repeat themselves with regularity.
>
> Tiny changes in one context can have a significant impact in another.
>
> Our current knowledge and expertise will not necessarily continue to suffice, because the systems we are part of are changing so rapidly.
>
> **(Heffernan, 2019)**

This means that the human capacity to adapt and respond to our current situation is becoming increasingly crucial.

In *Working with the Elephant*, I aim to approach and understand tools in light of this new, complex state of affairs and to describe approaches and methods that can help us enhance our awareness of the here-and-now and may lead to changes in behaviour.

Using the Book in Practice: Small, Concrete Steps

Working with the Elephant is a tribute to micro-acts. All the small things people do on a daily basis to prevent elephants from being ignored (and growing big) and to be able, gradually, to approach the elephants and begin to address them.

Tiny steps are crucial and often highly impactful. Many people lose courage and give up because the questions they ask seem too big and overwhelming. For example, 'How do I create a culture of psychological safety?' is an excellent question, but it is also a question that can quickly become too abstract or overwhelming.

In *Working with the Elephant*, we approach the big questions by taking small, concrete steps. The main thing is to do *something*. Having the feeling of moving forward, if ever so slightly, instead of remaining where we are or even taking a step back. Poking the issue a little, pushing a little, rocking the boat a little. A little is fine. In fact, it is good.

You can begin with those questions in the book that speak to you the most because they reflect the specific issues you are facing. Or you can choose to work through all of them, acknowledging the things you are already doing and taking inspiration from what you could choose to do more.

The Structure of the Book

Working with the Elephant grew out of the myriad curious and important questions that arise when we work with elephants. These questions have been condensed into the ten challenges that form the core of the workbook.

? Challenges

Challenge 1

What do I do when I miss important signals?

Challenge 2

What do I do when I avoid issues that make me feel insecure?

Challenge 3

What is my next step when I have entered uncertainty and decided to stay with the struggle?

Challenge 4

How do I address difficult issues?

Challenge 5

What do I do when there is no psychological safety?

Challenge 6

What do I do when power is present in the room?

Challenge 7

How do I deal with impression management and pretence?

Challenge 8

What do I do if I have become the designated elephant handler?

Challenge 9

How do I approach the big elephants that have been around for much too long?

Challenge 10

What is the appropriate timing and dosage for dealing with elephants?

Each challenge is introduced with my reflections on the core phenomenon addressed in the question. The purpose of this section is to examine the challenge and offer some perspectives that might be helpful to consider and to clarify the nature of the challenge.

Reflections

Next, under the heading of 'Reflections', I offer some thoughts that may help you get a clearer understanding of the challenge as it appears to you in your specific context.

Tips

Next, I offer some specific tips for your practice to support and enhance your capacity to reflect on and be mindful of the situation you are in. The tips are intended as actionable suggestions, but they should always be adapted to suit you and your context (which 'Reflections' helped you to consider in more detail).

My Own Pages

Each challenge is followed up with My Own Pages. In a sense, these are the most important pages in the workbook. This is where you write down what is most important for you to think about, stay with and/or act on. They also provide a simple structure to help you take action on the issues that are most important to you, your group or your joint task.

Use My Own Pages as you work your way through the book. Take notes when something interests you, hits home or makes you wonder – and write it down when you notice something new or when you are inspired to act on something that has been building up or just sitting in the back of your mind.

This is the structure of My Own Pages:

1. **Essential to me:**
   - What gets my attention?
   - What do I need to pay special attention to?
2. **Micro-acts I want to start with:**
   - What (small) step will I take?
   - When?
   - With whom?
   - What difference is it going to make (for me/the group/ our mission)?
   - How will I know that I am succeeding (what will be/ feel different in me /in the group/in relation to our mission)?

These are some of the most important pages in the book because, in many cases, the answer to whether something is the right or wrong thing to do in an organizational context is, 'It depends …'

Our world is complex. And approaching and dealing with elephants is no easy task. But it is also not an impossible one. The main thing is to make it as simple as possible. That journey begins with you.

In their book *Living Leadership: A Practical Guide for Ordinary Heroes* (2005), the researchers and leadership consultants George Binney, Gerhard Wilke and Colin Williams describe what makes for good leadership and good followership in a complex organizational context. Again, they do not offer simple answers, such as, 'If you simply …'.

No, what works is,

1. Get connected: Build openness and trust to address difficult issues openly.
2. Get real: Work with *what is – here and now.*

3. Know yourself: The better you know yourself, your choices and the consequences of your choices, the better you can bring yourself into play and have the influence you want.

Their recommendations are fully in line with my own experiences and research findings.

When you start by trying to get to know yourself better, you are starting in the right place. When you use your self-insight to take small steps and work with *what is*, you are on the right path …

My Own Pages invites you to connect with every challenge you face and consider the following:

How does it look from my perspective?
What do I recognize?
What should I pay attention to?
What do I want to act on?

Of course, some challenges will speak to you more than other challenges. So, go where your energy is.

Always remember that good learning is characterized by curiosity when things do not work out as you expected or hoped.

Rather than hitting yourself over the head when you fail, see if you can replace 'I should have …' with asking yourself

What just happened?
What did I notice?
What did I learn?
What do I want to pay attention to in the future?

This will make difficult learning processes more fun, easier and more effective!

I hope you will enjoy using My Own Pages. They are important, so remember to approach them with (self-) care and respect.

Before we get started on the challenges, I will outline the theoretical cornerstones underpinning *The Elephant in the Room* (2023).

Theoretical Cornerstones

The Unconscious Task Often Overrides the Conscious Task

Let me begin with a classic example from a decision-making process in a group.

A working group is having a disagreement. This may be anything from process issues, such as 'Should we do this together or in smaller groups?' to task-related questions, such as 'How many external stakeholders do we need to interview to get a picture of our clients' needs?'

Whenever there is a disagreement, 'Let's take a vote!' is a typical response. Equally typically, once this idea has been put on the table, the working group immediately proceeds to voting. This suggests that the idea appears immediately appealing. The question we should ask is,

> **What does the group *gain*, and what does it *lose* by opting for this approach?**

The benefits are obvious: The disagreement is quickly resolved, and the group can get on with its task. The group also avoids potentially drawn-out discussions, possible conflicts and the risk that some members will be angry and frustrated.

However, the group also loses something: Both the decision-making process and the quality of the decision suffer under this quick and easy solution. Minority voices risk being systematically ignored or overheard when the group favours a quick vote. Furthermore, the nuances of the different points of view are lost in this quick, quantitative solution. Nuances that it might be important to consider in order to reach the best possible decision.

As classic as the proposal and the immediate support for it are, the working group is typically equally quick to recognize that 'voting might not be the best solution' if it is made aware of the drawbacks at the moment.

So why do we choose this approach? Why does no one say, 'Hmm, are we sure this is the best solution? Perhaps we should listen to the different points of view before we proceed?'

The reason is that the unconscious task – in this case, *avoidance* of potential conflict – overrides the conscious task, which is to reach a well-founded decision. This happens in a split second and without anyone really noticing it. Even if some members might briefly connect with a feeling of avoidance, usually, they are quickly seduced by the unconscious task.

In *The Elephant in the Room*, I refer to the following quotation by Kim James and Tanya Arroba of the Cranfield School of Management:

> *The manager who can't understand why a perfectly good plan is not being executed may have few choices for intervening if s/he doesn't grasp that it is underwater rocks their ship has run into.*
>
> **(James & Arroba, 2005)**

To understand behaviours that do not appear to make sense and confusing paradoxes that call for a 'How come …?' – that is, all the things we defy understanding or explanation – we need to look under the surface. We need to be curious about the unconscious motives or what we might call *the unconscious task.*

In the opening example of the working group, we saw how unconscious motives drive the decision to take a vote. By engaging the unconscious and being curious about what is going on under the surface, we can gain a better understanding of all the aspects of organizational life that are otherwise hidden and do not seem to make sense.

We can practise looking for what lies just under the surface, pausing and curiously examining it, putting it into words, sharing it and trying to understand and find shared meaning in it.

Group Dynamics Are Always Present

A group is more than the sum of its individual members. Everything – and everyone – can only be understood in context. We are connected; we influence and shape each other, just as we are influenced and shaped by each other.

Group dynamics are usually complex and involve crisscross relations, some of them known, others unknown. When there is dissonance in cooperation and interactions, we can often improve our understanding by looking at *emotions, relationships* and *potential alliances.*

Let me provide an example of how a curious look at group dynamics under the surface might appear:

- In a board meeting, the board is discussing the possibility of adding a couple of younger members to the board, as they might offer a fresh look at some of the change processes the organization is facing. This is crucially important, as the board often finds itself paralysed and lacking insights and perspectives from the younger generation.

- Keith sees the need and – at a rational level – thinks it is a good idea. It might even be a necessary condition for the board to provide good governance. But he is also concerned: How would it affect his position on the board? As things stand, he is the main source of new perspectives. Would he be pushed aside and marginalized by the proposed new members?
- The proposal to bring in new and younger board members came from Mia. Keith perceives Mia as insecure and cautious. Perhaps even slightly incompetent? As a result, he tries to position himself as far away from Mia as possible to avoid being seen in the same light. Fred is more hesitant. Often, he also takes quite a conservative stand and is less open to change. However, Keith wants Fred to see him as a strong person (after all, Fred is the largest shareholder). 'I'm unsure,' says Fred. Keith feels anxious and concerned. 'I'm also not so sure it's a good idea,' says Keith.

The confounding observation is, 'Why is there such doubt about something that, on its face, seems like an excellent idea and a necessary step?' In this situation, we need to try to understand the dynamics at play under the surface.

The conscious task in this case is to make the board more qualified. The unconscious task is to secure a strong position in the internal competition and to appear certain and competent. We know (because we know what is happening in Keith under the surface) that Keith is trying to solve the unconscious task by distancing himself from Mia (whom he sees as the weaker card) and allying himself with Fred (whom he considers the stronger card). We do not know what is at stake for the other members, but we can pause and adopt a curious stance.

It is important to consider group dynamics and to have a conceptual basis for seeking to understand them. Otherwise, we run a number of risks:

> One is the risk of oversimplifying a complex reality and therefore taking unqualified decisions. In the example above, this would be a quick decision based mainly on avoiding potential competition among the existing members rather than a well-founded decision that addresses the challenge at hand.

Another risk is that of holding individuals responsible for complex situations that are co-created in and by the group. In this case, Mia is positioned as 'incompetent' – not because she is, but because it lets Keith distance himself from the uncomfortable feeling of incompetence and instead position himself as competent.

When we take a curious look at group dynamics, we distinguish between formal roles, which are determined by the group's main task, and the psychodynamic roles that develop in the interaction and which the group members (often unconsciously) assign to each other.

Valency

Our roles are determined by ourselves, the other group members and the group's needs for having certain roles filled. The British psychoanalyst Wilfred Bion (1968) argued that we tend to take on certain roles that meet our inner needs. He called this tendency *valence*.

For example, if someone has valence for acting as a conflict mediator (perhaps because they grew up as a middle child in a highly conflicted family), this role may be highly desirable for a group with many conflicts, and thus, the person may, more or less consciously, take on or be assigned that role. If the group changes, the person's role will change too.

If someone has valence for letting their voice be heard, they may take on or be assigned the role of being the one who speaks up in the group. Others who do not have similar valence can lean back and let this person carry that particular responsibility on behalf of the group.

When someone has valence for a particular role, they will often slip into this role unconsciously. Once they become aware of it, they may find themselves wondering, 'What just happened? How did I end up taking the responsibility – and the risk – on behalf of the others?'

Now imagine that the person who, for example, has valence for speaking up in the group were to leave the group. What will happen to the group when this role is no longer filled? How will this affect the members who left it to the former member to put the difficult and conflicted issues into words?

What the group deposited in this person now 'reverts to' the group. It is easy to imagine that this will result in turmoil, positioning and power struggles.

Emotions Are Data

In 2009, the Belgian artist Thomas Leeroy made a series of bronze sculptures titled 'Not Enough Brain to Survive'. The sculptures are powerful, dramatic and emotional. Take a little time just to observe the sculpture and take it in (Figure 0.1).

What thoughts and feelings arise in you?
What associations does the sculpture spark in you?
How does it speak to you?

Figure 0.1 The sculpture 'Not Enough Brain to Survive' by Thomas Leeroy.

To me, it speaks to our tendency to overfocus on thinking, overemphasizing the rational decision-making process which promises that if we only gather enough information, we will find the right answer.

We have been raised to accept the significance of thinking. We are also rated and evaluated on our ability to put our thoughts into words, to analyse and to understand. The risk is that we let our bodies and emotions slip into the background. That we neglect our ability to sense and notice – 'What am I feeling right now?' – and that we do not view emotions as valid data that are worth relating to and taking into consideration.

Many of us are so used to 'being in our heads' that we might struggle to answer the questions, 'What are you feeling right now?' and 'How are you feeling?' The most common answer is 'I feel fine.'

'Fine' or 'Good' or 'Okay' may describe how we feel, but what does it actually mean? 'Fine' is not a feeling. The way 'Fine' is said may cover over a wide range of emotions: Worried, scared, inadequate, embarrassed, disappointed, vulnerable, frustrated, annoyed, bitter, disoriented, surprised, proud, strong, satisfied, happy …

The question 'What are you feeling right now?' is a well-known exercise for training emotional intelligence and enhancing the capacity to draw on emotional data.

One reason why emotions are perceived as vague or difficult to put into words is our inclination to view emotions as less relevant than thoughts. Some emotions may even be viewed as dangerous, disturbing, difficult or messy; hence the inclination to avoid them. However, the more we avoid them, the more dangerous they tend to seem, because avoidance prevents us from understanding them. Instead, we treat them as something to be pushed aside or eliminated, especially in contexts where we would like our emotions to appear a little more streamlined, as is often the case in the workplace. As a result, emotions as a form of intelligence, as important sources of information and as data often slip into the background.

When we clean up our emotions or stop paying attention to them, we miss out on a lot of important information – about ourselves and others, about the here-and-now and about the there-and-then. Because emotions are an important source of understanding what is at play in human interactions – there and then as well as here and now.

When we use emotions as data, we adopt a curious stance towards the perceived emotion at several levels:

Inner level

> How am I feeling right now?
> Why might that be?
> What triggers this emotions?
> What belongs to me, what belongs to someone else?
> How does this emotion affect me right now in terms of the actions I take and the decisions I make?

Outer level

> What does this emotion tell me about what is happening right here, right now, in the group that I am part of?
> What is not just about me but about the group?
> How can this emotion help me understand what is going on right now?

In the example with the board, let us imagine that instead of avoiding his feeling of anxiety or concern, Keith stays with them for a moment and allows them to inform his decision-making. That his 'I'm also not so sure that it's a good idea' is followed up by reflection and a question, such as 'I too feel a certain anxiety and concern with regard to this decision – and maybe I'm not the only one. Perhaps we could look into what might be a concern when it comes to taking in new members as well as not doing it?'

Defences Should Be Embraced

Most of us are familiar with the urge to explain our intentions or rationalize our actions when we receive feedback that we find difficult to take in. Deep down, we also know that the more we explain, defend, rationalize and intellectualize, the harder it may be to listen to someone else's perception and message. These defences simply stand in the way of our ability to understand someone else's experience and where the person is coming from.

Defences are necessary and exist for a reason, but it takes mindful attention to determine when they are necessary and helpful and when they are getting in the way of development and learning – for individuals, groups and organizations. Moreover, many of our defences are unconscious. That is why organizational psychologists often describe defences as one of their main challenges.

Defences also include inner dialogues – plausible stories which we use to explain, rationalize and intellectualize to ourselves why it might be 'a good idea' to give an elephant in the room a wide berth. Getting to know our own defences, so that we can recognize the less helpful ones, is a key factor when working with elephants.

Just as we need to get to know our own defences, it is also helpful to learn more about our responses to *other people's* defences. Encountering others' defences can often cause irritation or animosity, which may get in the way of curious investigation – and curiosity is essential to maintain.

For now, let us take a quick look at some common defence mechanisms and the typical responses they elicit.

Some of the responses we often encounter are denial, intellectualization and humour.

It is fairly easy to understand why denial in particular can be intensely provoking to others. It is difficult to enter into a dialogue about something that one person denies but which the other person might find fairly obvious. Because intellectualization is often perceived as distancing and as a denial of accountability, it can be perceived as provoking and as an obstacle to engagement and accountability. Humour can offer relief, but it may also seem inappropriate and unsafe if it gives the impression that difficult or serious issues are taken lightly.

It is important to maintain our curiosity despite any animosity and irritation we might feel. What does the defence represent? How does it arise, and why is it perceived as necessary?

If we understand what triggers the defensive response, we are better able to put the other person at ease. This makes it possible to talk about issues that are difficult but essential to address.

CHALLENGE 1

DOI: 10.4324/9781003582939-1

What Do I Do When I Miss Important Signals?

• *Double awareness* • *Tunnel vision as automatic behaviour* • *The competence trap* • *We are all always seeing something* • *Addiction to action* • *Amygdala hijacks versus mindfulness*

During a presentation for executives, one (brave) leader asked me,

'What if I don't notice anything in the situation? What if I only really notice something while I'm in my car, on my way home? Or if I only really notice the signals when others draw my attention to them after the fact? Then what? That makes it hard to act on what I notice in the moment.'

This is true. The first step is always to spot, notice, wonder about something ... And while we are in the midst of it all, our awareness of ourselves and others often may have a tendency to slip into the background.

Any organizational process contains two coexisting tracks, which the English psychoanalyst and organizational consultant Harold Bridger (and one of the founders of the Tavistock Institute) labelled Task 1 and Task 2.

One track is focused on the activity itself: *What* we are working on, as a group (Task 1). The other track is focused on relational and processual aspects: *How* we are working

DOI: 10.4324/9781003582939-1

together (Task 2). It is a well-known challenge that when the pace is increased, deadlines are looming, and e-mails are pouring in, our attention on Task 2 begins to slip, as we devote more attention to Task 1.

When we manage to alternate smoothly between Task 1 and Task 2, being simultaneously aware of *what* we are doing and *how* we are doing it, we successfully practise what I call *double awareness.*

There are benefits to maintaining an intense mission focus, as it may represent concentrated, focused and consistent attention to Task 1, which promotes the efficient accomplishment of the work at hand. However, if it causes you to lose awareness of yourself, the people around you and the situation you are part of, resulting in one-track tunnel vision, there is a price to pay: You miss out on information, alternative points of view, new perspectives and so forth. When you are mainly focused on your own individual task, you overlook other important aspects, including 'What do the others think? Where might they contribute relevant perspectives? What uncertainties do they have that I might help them with? What are my uncertainties that they might help me with?'

The data you fail to pick up on hold a wealth of missed information, possibilities and ideas. Your work performance, creativity and innovation will suffer when you fail to take in and examine new angles and ideas.

This situation risks leading to what Chris Argyris, professor of organizational theory, aptly describes as *the competence trap*: The more successful you are at your job, the less able you are to see alternatives, because you rely on your own rationalization of legitimacy. You also risk losing your sense of connectedness.

Losing your sense of connectedness not only leads to a feeling of loneliness. You also lose sense of what is happening in and between the groups you are part of. This makes it harder to navigate in decision-making and collaboration processes, because you have so little sense of what is happening. There is also a risk of unnoticed emotional data building up, including signals of stress and a lack of well-being. That was the case for the manager who asked this question. Suddenly, there were mountains in front of him that he had to climb, and which he totally had not anticipated.

To some, a one-sided focus on Task 1 becomes a habit based on the conscious or unconscious conviction that failing to maintain a constant mission focus will lead to a loss of momentum and results. While the conscious task in this case is a focus on the job at hand, the potential unconscious task is avoiding the potential complexity of collaboration and human interaction. We avoid complexity by focusing exclusively on what we can control. This diminishes our capacity to be in and with Task 2. When tunnel vision becomes a habit – what we do, our comfort zone – challenging the habit can be a challenge in itself (see Challenge 4).

However, the question, 'What if I don't notice it in the moment?' invites an important counter-question: 'Is it *actually* the case that you don't see it? Or do you actually see it more than you are immediately aware of (perhaps because you simply have trouble distinguishing what you notice)?' We are all always seeing something!

As part of my research, I have observed groups while they worked on their main task. During my observations, I gathered concrete behavioural data: What was said, done, expressed and so forth. Afterwards, I spoke with each of the group members. In these conversations, I gathered a different type of data: What they had thought, felt and assumed, and was able to probe and be curious about the thoughts that had been shared and the ones that had not been shared. This revealed a significant and interesting phenomenon: I was genuinely surprised to see how much the individual group members picked up on, noticed and had feelings and thoughts about that were not expressed in the group. The group picked up many more process signals than they addressed – and many more than I thought. Thus, as I briefly mentioned in the Introduction, the question in my mind during my observations – 'How come they are not noticing this?' – was not the right question.

This means that it is likely that you pick up on more than you might think but push it aside so quickly that you tell yourself that 'I am not actually picking up the signals.' The challenge, therefore, has as much to do with mindful avoidance as with 'not noticing anything'. Thus, the real question becomes, 'Is it the case that I miss the signals – or is it, rather, that I choose (consciously or unconsciously) not to see them?'

The challenge may also be that you end up devoting a lot of energy to keeping unwanted and complicated signals out (I address this issue in Challenge 2).

When the real challenge is that you fail to pick up the signals, the question is how you can begin to tune into the signals that – for whatever reason – tend to evade your radar. That question is related to the question about how you can develop and enhance both your self-insight and your social insight.

HOW CAN I BEGIN TO PICK UP THE SIGNALS THAT I DO NOT NOTICE?

So, how can you begin to notice what is happening inside you, between you and other people, between other people and in the group as a whole, *while you work* on your shared main task?

This challenge could also be described as, 'How do I make sure that I also focus on Task 2 without losing myself completely in Task 1?' The question, 'How do I know if this is avoidance behaviour?' is addressed under Challenge 2.

POINTS FOR REFLECTION

Efficiency Can Undermine Your Capacity to Pick Up on Emotional Data

We are programmed for speed and to 'think' rather than to 'feel'. That is why we need to actively train our awareness to slow down – and to orient more towards emotional data. To offer a simple metaphor: When you walk slowly and look up, you create the conditions for noticing many more details around you than when you run. Sometimes you have to slow down in order to get to your destination faster. If you overlook data along the way, you may have to backtrack more than once in order to pick up what you missed.

The main step to take here is simply to consider when and with whom can you practise slowing down in order to practise picking up the signals you might otherwise tend to miss.

Addiction to Action and Pseudo-Efficiency (Inefficiently) Increases the Pace Even More

Also note when you are being 'efficient' simply because it feels good to be 'doing something' but what you achieve is not actually very meaningful. We often call this 'pseudo-efficiency' or 'busywork,' which is a form of addiction to action, where 'doing something' becomes an end in itself. This carries a significant risk of getting stuck in one-track tunnel vision with a narrow focus on Task 1 but with busyness as the actual purpose. Most of us recognize pseudo-efficiency in the form of unproductive multitasking or unnecessary meetings, where the pace prevents us from pausing, questioning what we are doing, and making sure it is meaningful.

If you feel you are constantly busy, the first thing you need to do is stop and ask yourself whether all the things you are doing actually generate meaning for yourself and others.

Contradictory Signals Should Not Be Fixed but Met with Curiosity

Signals are often contradictory and confusing. For example, you may have a colleague who says 'yes' while their body language say 'no' when you make a request. In many cases, when you pick up contradictory and confusing signals, the source of the confusion is not that you are unable to pick up meaningful signals or make sense of the confusing signals you pick up. Instead, it simply occurs because the signals *are* mixed. In this situation, remind yourself that your primary task is *not* to make sense of what you pick up. All you need to do is be curious about what you see and notice – including contradictory signals.

In groups, there will often be contradictory and confusing signals. For example, take a curious look at the following example from *The Elephant in the Room* (2023), and pay attention to what signals you pick up. Perhaps you actually pick up more signals than you think, but do not attribute them much importance in relation to the main task your group is working on.

What signals do you pick up in the following example? And what potential consequences do you see in ignoring them?

A group is working on a business challenge. The group members are under pressure. They have a lot to accomplish and a limited amount of time. After first attempting to develop an overview of their common task, they try to make a plan to ensure an efficient group process. The planning is proving difficult.

Stan: 'We need a plan for the remainder of today and tomorrow!'

Shirley: 'Should we make the plan together, or should we split up?'
Stan: 'It'll just take 10 minutes.'
Shirley: 'Okay?'

She raises her eyebrows and looks at Stan. Stan ignores her. The group begins to discuss tomorrow's task in detail. They address various elements of the task, but fail to reach any conclusions.

Shirley says, 'But now we're doing it in *10* minutes!' She emphasizes '10'. With obvious irritation and irony in her voice. Then she smiles. Stan does not reply. A new question is raised, and the group discussion resumes. Shirley closes her eyes and rests her head in her hands. Stan closes his eyes and begins to massage his forehead.

One of the group members is not taking part in the discussion. He does not make eye contact with any of the others, but opens his laptop and begins to type.

Perhaps he is replying to e-mails? None of the other group members speaks to him or takes any interest in what he is doing.

Your Primary Task Is to Practise Mindfulness

Mindfulness is a way to be more connected to the moment by devoting your full attention to what you are doing right here and right now, whatever it is; mindful of what is happening around you as well as inside you. Practising mindfulness can help you become aware of your own patterns and mindsets – including the ones that are not helpful or which get in the way of what you want to do.

> *Mindfulness is the awareness that emerges through paying attention on purpose, in the present moment, and non-judgmentally to things as they are. Pay attention to what? you might ask. To anything, but especially to those aspects of life that we most take for granted or ignore.*
>
> **(Mark Williams et al., 2008, p. 55)**

Think of mindfulness as your primary task! And practise doing it right here-and-now: I want to be fully present and notice what is happening in me and around me in this present moment.

Remind yourself that this is your task. Your task is not to rate anything as either good or bad or to fix what is not working.

It Is Never Too Late

What you notice after the fact, as you are driving home from work, for example, can be addressed the next time you encounter it. You can always go back.

TIPS

Test Your Addiction to Action

For example, do you get started on the first thing that happens to catch your attention when you sit down at your desk? An e-mail? A problem that pops up? If you see signs of addiction to action in yourself, give yourself a moment's pause in between stimulus and response to make a proactive decision about what it makes sense for you to address.

Find a Mindfulness Practice that Works for You

Mindfulness practice includes both formal and informal training. While formal training consists of breaks where you place mindfulness at the centre, for example via meditation, informal training is integrated into your daily activities as you practise mindfulness as part of doing something else: For example, by bringing your full attention to drinking coffee, savouring and enjoying it; by walking from one place to another with full attention on your movement and whatever you encounter along the way; or by having a meeting with someone and bringing your full attention to bear on the other person, yourself and your mutual interaction.

Practising mindfulness does not require you to change what you do; what it implies is *a shift in your attention to what you are doing*. Your focus is on being mindful of what you are doing, as you are doing it. This is not about behavioural change but about applying curiosity and attention to the here-and-now.

One helpful guide is *The Mindful Way Workbook: An 8-Week Program to Free Yourself from Depression and Emotional Distress* by the three psychology and mindfulness scholars John Teasdale, Mark Williams and Zindel Segal (2013). You can follow this programme from start to finish or choose the elements that make sense for you.

Slow Down and Increase Your Focus on Task 2 – One Small Step at a Time

Decide when, how and with whom you want to practise this capacity on a daily basis.

Explore When You Might Be at Heightened Risk of Amygdala Hijack

When we are challenged, facing difficulties or dealing with unfamiliar or confusing situations, we need mindfulness more than ever. When you have built up your capacity for mindfulness in everyday situations, try applying it in difficult or challenging situations. When you are under pressure, the amygdala in your brain is activated, which puts you at heightened risk of amygdala hijack. In this situation, we react with automatic behaviours, often characterized by fight or flight responses.

Notice what or who is most likely to hijack you, and try to practise mindfulness in these situations as well:

- Note your own emotions. And ask what others are feeling.
- Read novels or short stories with particular attention to signals in interpersonal interactions.

Notice the Subtle Signals

Christian Jungersen's novel *The Exception* (2006) revolves around the relationship between three coworkers. Their interactions contain a wealth of subtle signals that can be interpreted and understood in many different ways. Try to notice all the subtle signals.

Then look at the signals that no one examines or asks about and which instead become the basis of speculation. Read the book – or watch the film – with particular focus on avoidance behaviour. Notice the things that are not said, asked or questioned. Notice what this behaviour does to the culture and relationships. Although events in *The Exception* go beyond what happens in an average workplace, most of us will still recognize certain aspects – those little things that we do not have any data for but which form the basis of speculation about what others are like or why they do what they do.

Train Your Capacity to Be in the Here-and-Now in the Midst of It All

Even while there is a lot going on that you are involved in and need to be in and relate to train your capacity to be in the here-and-now. Take part in group relations conferences, where the participants work together to build learning organizations that explore what is happening in themselves, between the individual members, and in the group as a whole. This offers an opportunity to practise noticing (and acting on what you notice) in complex situations and interpersonal relationships.

Train Your Capacity to Listen to Yourself and Your Own Signals

Take part in silent retreats. In a silent retreat, you reduce the noise around you, which lets you listen more closely to what is happening inside you. This gives you intense training in listening to those signals inside you that may go unnoticed most of the time. It also serves as an opportunity to practise intensive mindfulness.

MY OWN PAGES

Essential to Me

What gets my attention?

What do I need to pay special attention to?

Micro-Acts I Want to Start With

What (small) step will I take?

When?

With whom?

What difference is it going to make (for me/the group/our mission)?

How will I know that I am succeeding (what will be/feel different in me/in the group/in relation to our mission)?

CHALLENGE

2

DOI: 10.4324/9781003582939-2

What Do I Do When I Avoid Issues That Make Me Feel Insecure?

• Avoidance behaviour • Comfort zone as hiding place • Plausible stories as a defence • Mindful avoidance • Sphere of interest and powerlessness • Continuous training • A personalized early warning system • Nothing is too small

Like the leader in Challenge 1, you may find that even as you practise being mindful, slowing down and picking up your own and others' signals, you are also quickly and automatically letting the signals pass. In that case, you are practising mindful avoidance behaviour – and that is another specific challenge. You notice things but quickly render them unnoticed, because for some reason, they feel unsettling or potentially threatening.

In the comfort zone, everything is familiar and recognizable. This is not necessarily where we find what makes us happy or feels most meaningful, but it does offer a form of familiarity that contributes to a sense of security. Habits, routines ... all the things we know we are well equipped to deal with.

DOI: 10.4324/9781003582939-2

Sometimes we need to leave our comfort zone and move into the learning zone. Familiar and safe are not necessarily what makes us happy or which works for us.

We may need to do this because we find ourselves in a new situation or because a familiar situation has become untenable or unbearable. This calls for us to do something other than what we normally do. Perhaps there will be negative consequences if we do not – for ourselves, the group we are part of or our shared task. The moment when we step outside our comfort zone is a vulnerable moment because we move from the familiar to the unfamiliar, from certainty to uncertainty. This step is often associated with concern and anxiety because we might worry about the consequences. Once you realize that you may have a tendency to retreat when you approach the edge of your comfort zone and then begin to delve into what keeps you from leaving it, you also begin to be curious about your own unconscious autopilot behaviour. That lets you explore what you do, which in turn can enable you to engage with what you choose to focus on. This is not an easy process, and it requires a willingness to deal with things that may feel difficult.

When we approach the edge of our comfort zone, the human psyche shows extraordinary creativity when it comes to finding ways and *telling (plausible) stories* to help us stay in our comfort zone as long as possible. This is an unconscious way of protecting ourselves from the feeling of risk associated with entering less familiar territory. However, the stories we tell ourselves – such as 'It's better to wait until tomorrow' or 'It won't make any difference anyway' – are not always helpful. They are unhelpful when they prevent us from moving on or taking the steps we would like to be able to take, or when they confirm the idea that we are only competent and safe as long as we stay in our comfort zone. They are also unhelpful when they contribute to short-sighted decisions that are driven mainly by avoidance rather than by what would be best for you, for others and for the task at hand, also in the long term. In that situation, the comfort zone is not a good place to be. On the contrary, in the long term, it may become a risky place: A hideaway that no longer functions as intended.

One example of a hideaway that no longer functions as intended would be someone who stays quiet in meetings to avoid saying something stupid. This person stays quiet in order to protect themselves from potential exposure of ignorance. Paradoxically, however, this makes them a projection screen for others' assumptions and imagination. A common assumption is that the quiet person is quiet because they have nothing meaningful to contribute. In this case, the hideaway no longer works as intended – on the contrary.

HOW DO I RECOGNIZE THE LESS HELPFUL STORIES I TELL MYSELF WHICH PREVENT ME FROM ACTING ON WHAT I NOTICE?

The stories we tell ourselves may sound fairly plausible, and that is exactly what makes them so difficult to deal with. They are easy to buy into. In the moment, it is simply more comfortable to accept them. We have an automatic tendency to accept easy and plausible stories that allow us to retreat to our comfort zone without even noticing it. To further complicate matters, sometimes it actually is a fine idea to wait until tomorrow. In other words, how do we know when we are turning to avoidance behaviour and when waiting is actually the best policy? When should we listen to the voice that tells us to wait, and when should we challenge it? Where do we draw the line?

Let us look at an example:

Christian has a couple of coworkers who are generally quite dominating. They walk over others and cut people off in conversations. In the open-plan office, they are not very attentive to others but talk a lot and laugh loudly. Christian finds them intensely annoying. They are a nuisance, especially when he needs to concentrate or has conversations with clients.

Whenever he even thinks about broaching the issue, his heart starts racing, and his palms get clammy. The thought makes him uncomfortable: 'What if they find me intolerant and overly sensitive? I'm probably the only person who has a problem with their behaviour,' he tells himself. 'I should just get better at concentrating on my work and ignoring the distractions. If I bring it up, they will probably think I'm too touchy. I don't want to risk a conflict since we are seated so close together.'

Christian does not say anything. His clammy palms return to normal. His coworkers continue chatting.

Did Christian do the right thing – from the perspectives of his own well-being, his coworkers and his work task? Should he challenge the stories he tells himself (Might they be avoidance strategies?), or should he take them at face value, as he does in the example? What do you think?

The most accurate answer to this question is found inside Christian. *If* the problem remains equally pressing the rest of the day, *if* he finds himself going over the situation on his way home from work – 'I should have said something ...' or 'Someone should have done something about it' – and *if* he recognizes some of the characteristic emotions associated with mindful avoidance: A heavy feeling, self-blame, a sense of self-betrayal and so forth. This indicates that it would be helpful to address his experience and the impact it has on his ability to focus and concentrate on his work.

POINTS FOR REFLECTION

Examine the Stories You Tell Yourself from a Position of Curiosity and Kindness

When we get close to the edge of our comfort zone, we need to be especially alert and attentive. If not, we will automatically accept the easy, plausible story that allows us to return to our comfort zone – without even noticing it. The leader who asked the question that was described in Challenge 1 – 'What if I don't notice anything in the situation? That makes it hard to act on what I notice in the moment' – was also bravely examining his own avoidance strategies. He wanted to get better at picking up signals, but he was also asking himself, '*Am* I really incapable of noticing anything?' The answer was, 'No, I *do* pick up signals, but avoiding them has become my comfort zone.'

Avoid asking yourself questions in a self-evaluating or self-blaming form. Instead, aim to practise kindness, curiosity and mindfulness towards yourself.

Get to Know Your Avoidance Strategies – the Typical Stories You Tell Yourself

In his TED Talk 'Building Essential Collaborative Skills', the former judge and conflict resolution expert Jim Tamm, who is also the coauthor of *Radical Collaboration* (2004), offers one very simple piece of advice: 'Stop being so defensive.'

According to Tamm, nothing is going to do more to improve your capacity for cooperation and conflict resolution than that. But he is also aware that it is not easy to do. Precisely because the human psyche is going to strive to make the uncomfortable situation bearable and protect us from anything we might be afraid of and would prefer not to connect with. To that end, it provides defensive stories for us to lean on and avoid those emotions.

In my research, I generally encounter four significant avoidance stories that we commonly tell ourselves:

- It is better not to reveal how I feel; the group probably cannot handle it.
- I need to be careful not to get caught up in something I cannot control (emotions), so I will quickly move on if there are too many emotions at play.
- If I cannot resolve the issue in the situation or fix what is wrong, it is better to leave things alone.
- I'm probably the only one who feels this way, so I don't want to bother the others with it.

Becoming familiar with your typical avoidance stories can help you recognize and spot them in the midst of everything that is going on. Perhaps you recognize one or more of the four avoidance stories – and perhaps there is a fifth story that is more significant to you. Be curious about the stories you tell yourself:

- What are your stories? What stories do you typically tell yourself: Stories that do not help you but convince you that it is a good idea for you to stay inside your comfort zone?
- What are you defending against? What are you most afraid of (Not being important? Not being competent? Not being liked by others? Something else entirely?)?
- What do your stories help you to avoid?

When the leader who asked, 'What if I don't notice anything?' (Challenge 1), examines the stories he tells himself, he accepts the story that goes, 'If I don't know how to fix what I notice it's better to pretend I don't notice it.' And when he dwells on a particular moment, he realizes that this is an example of avoidance behaviour rather than incapacity to pick up the signals. He also realizes that as a leader, he feels responsible for fixing anything related to his employees' well-being rather than seeing it as a shared issue that it is up to the group, as a whole, to work out.

Thus, he inadvertently places a huge burden on his own shoulders.

If You Place Yourself Outside Your Own Sphere of Influence, You Accept Your Own Powerlessness

Think of the potential consequences of Christian's decision to stay silent.

Christian has an interest in having a working environment where coworkers are considerate of each other, speak softly or take their conversations elsewhere and are generally respectful of each other's needs, especially when someone is on the phone with a client or is working on something that requires their full focus and attention.

However, through the stories he tells himself, he *places himself outside his own sphere of influence* and gives up his own needs and wants.

In your sphere of interest, your orientation is reactive, and your position is defensive: It is someone else's fault, there is nothing you can do and it really does not matter. Once you enter the sphere of influence, your orientation is creative, and some of the key questions are: 'What do I want to create for myself and for the people I work with? What can I do to make that happen?' Or, simply put, 'What can I do to help build the sort of culture I would like to be part of?'

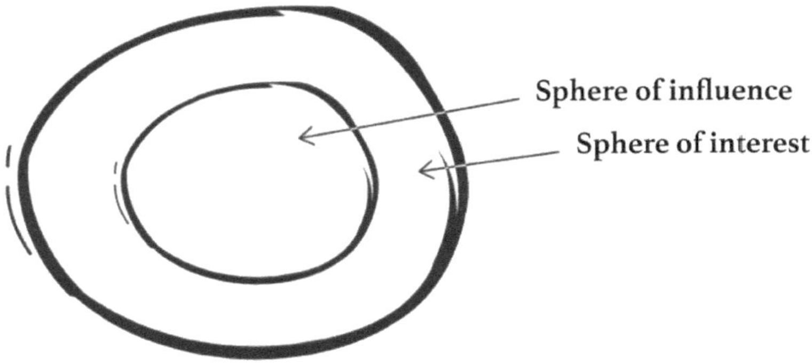

Figure 2.1 Our sphere of interest is defined as conditions we cannot change but have an interest in. Our sphere of influence is defined as conditions we can take responsibility for and which we can change.

Courage Involves Stepping Forward Despite Anxiety and Concern

Your strongest weapon when you want to get better at stepping outside your comfort zone is to be curious and explore what you are afraid of, rather than trying to make it go away. Courage is *not* the same as *not* feeling any anxiety or concern. Courage is the ability to step forward *despite* anxiety and concerns. As with anything else, the more you do it, the better you get at it. Think of it as psychological core training.

Persistent Training Is the Way

When things begin to feel slightly uncomfortable, you will know that you are moving out of your comfort zone. Every time that happens, you are improving your ability to step outside your comfort zone. Just as you do not build muscle strength by going to the fitness centre once and then thinking, 'Great, that was that,' your psychological core also does not grow strong through a single experience. It takes persistent training.

TIPS

Create a Personalized Early Warning System

In his TED Talk 'Building Essential Collaborative Skills', Jim Tamm recommends developing what he calls a 'personalized early warning system'. It can help you spot the defensive stories that pull you back inside your comfort zone when you approach your learning zone. Such an early warning system might include the following awareness:

> As I approach the edge of my comfort zone, I breathe faster, my heart beats faster, my palms get clammy, and I begin to talk faster.

By identifying these physical reactions as part of your early warning system, when you feel them, you will know that you have a heightened risk of buying into a defensive story. When that is the case, you need to be more alert, take a deep breath and make an active decision to stay with it.

Find One Small Step That Can Take You Out of Your Defensive Story – Out of Your Comfort Zone and Into Your Learning Zone

Next step is what Jim Tamm calls, 'Create an action step and practise it.' For Christian in the example, this could look as follows:

> My heart is beating faster, and my palms are getting clammy. This is a warning signal, telling me that something is important to me and that I need to take it seriously. THIS is when I need to stay with the struggle, rather than stepping back, and act on what I notice. What small step can I take right now?

Look for Low-Hanging Fruit: Small Steps are Important Steps

Nothing is too small. In fact, it is important not to take too big a step. It is like testing the ice on a frozen lake: You do not rush in and make a big jump. You move out step by tiny step, and even if the ice creaks a little, you remain confident that it will hold. Your chance of success is much greater if you take small steps – you can always take more.

The key is to keep moving forward, rather than staying where you are or stepping back.

Practise Being Mindful in the Midst of It All

Pause and ask yourself: What is happening right now? What am I thinking? What am I feeling? What would I like to have happen? What am I doing to prevent myself from getting what I want? Take a deep breath – and move on. (Rick Ross in Senge, 1994).

MY OWN PAGES

Essential To Me

What gets my attention?

What do I need to pay special attention to?

Micro-Acts I Want to Start With

What (small) step will I take?

When?

With whom?

What difference is it going to make (for me/the group/our mission)?

How will I know that I am succeeding (what will be/feel different in me/in the group/in relation to our mission)?

CHALLENGE

3

DOI: 10.4324/9781003582939-3

yes please

What Is My Next Step When I Have Entered Uncertainty and Decided To Stay with the Struggle?

• Negative capability • Creating a gap between stimulus and response • Assumptions about 'what will happen' • Fix versus curiosity • Psychological safety • Acknowledge and invite • Hold onto the main task • 'It's cold, so what?' • Routines and support structures • Compassion, humility, curiosity

Now you have successfully developed your own personalized early warning system (see Challenge 2). You have learnt to recognize the stories you tell yourself that may – unhelpfully – draw you away from discomfort and back into your comfort zone. And finally, you have managed to stay on the ice despite the creaking.

There you are now, on the creaking ice. In the midst of complexity, not-knowing, uncertainty and doubt. Now what? The short, simple answer is, 'Stay there!'

DOI: 10.4324/9781003582939-3

By staying, you train your sought-after and important negative capability: The ability and capacity to accept uncertainty and doubt, to stay with the complexity and the unknown, where there are no clear paths or answers, only not-knowing and uncertainty. Negative capability is the ability to stay with and contain the struggle until you begin to see a path that feels right, instead of retreating or quickly turning to arbitrary action to make your feelings of uncertainty and doubt go away.

Lisa is the head of a working group with many conflicts. Whenever she feels a conflict developing, her cheeks get hot, and she gets a sinking feeling in her stomach. Her autopilot reaction is to avoid the struggle by picking up the pace and directing attention away from relational aspects and towards the technical aspects of the group's task.

Lisa is now seeking to improve her ability to stay with the conflict instead of steering away from it. Her personalized early warning system is triggered by hot cheeks and a sinking feeling in her stomach. When she senses these reactions, she knows that she needs to remain mindful and do the opposite of her usual automatic behaviour by slowing down. So she takes a deep breath, looks up – and stays with it.

So the first step is to stay with what is happening. Some of the work in dealing with Challenges 1 and 2 involves understanding your own patterns, gaining insight into your own assumptions about and reactions to various situations. When you find yourself in the midst of it all and can feel the ice creaking, your main challenge is to create a small gap between stimulus and response to prevent an amygdala hijack or a flight-or-fight response and enable yourself to ask the questions described under Challenge 2:

What is happening right now? What am I thinking? What am I feeling? What would I like to have happen?

Let us return to the example of Christian and the open-plan office from Challenge 2.

After fuming in his car on his way home from work, frustrated that he did not say anything to his coworkers, Christian returns to work the following day. The situation is unchanged, and Christian takes an initial step onto the ice: 'When you have conversations in here, it is difficult for me to concentrate. Could you keep your voices down a little?' Now Christian is standing on the ice.

One of the coworkers looks at him, a little startled: 'Okay! We could go into one of the meeting rooms, I guess?'

This is a critical moment, involving discomfort, uncertainty and difficulty for Christian, who is worried about offending his coworkers and having them dislike him or find him difficult. Thus, his autopilot response would be, 'No, don't worry about, it's fine – you don't need to leave.' However, by staying with this feeling for a little longer, tolerating the discomfort and checking in with what would be the best for him, Christian is able to say, 'Yes, that would be very helpful! Thank you!'

Next step for Christian is to explore, 'Will people actually dislike me if I ...?'

HOW CAN I STAY WITH COMPLEXITY AND UNCERTAINTY WITHOUT LOSING MY FOOTING?

When we encounter difficulty, everything in us wants to take us somewhere else where things are easier.

All the questions in this challenge revolve around the same main issue: How can I make peace with not-knowing? How can I make peace with the unknown? How can I strengthen my psychological core? The key is to build resilience to be able to stay with not-knowing, difficulty, conflicts and so forth and to resist autopilot responses and amygdala hijacks.

POINTS FOR REFLECTION

One Form of Understanding Will Lead to One Form of Action

A quick experiment: Connect all nine dots with four straight lines without lifting your pencil from the paper (it is okay for lines to cross each other).[1] Try before you continue reading!

Many people assume that the lines have to stay inside the frame defined by the nine dots. However, that assumption would make the task impossible. So, where does it come from?

Assumptions Can Be Tested since They Are Just That: Assumptions

One form of understanding will lead to one form of action. Recognizing the connection between assumption and action can lead to new ways of organizing.

Assumptions arise in one place and spread to other contexts.

Test Your Assumptions about the World

Building negative capability should include testing your assumptions about 'what will happen'. For example, Christian is worried that his coworkers in the open-plan office will distance themselves from him and like him less if he asks them to speak more softly in the shared office space. He has a deep-seated assumption – and fear – that he will be excluded. This fear is the real obstacle for Christian, and he arrived at the task of defining it by asking himself, 'What is it I am *actually* afraid of?'

Christian's next step is to examine whether people actually *are* going to like him less and exclude him from the office community *when* he holds on to what is important to him. To determine that, he can look out for specific data, including whether they are going to speak to him less often, include him less, ask him fewer questions and so forth. With this approach, he is going to the root of what is keeping him from stepping up, rather than remaining passive (see *Immunity to Change* (Kegan & Lahey, 2009)).

The purpose of a test is to gather data about deep-seated assumptions you might hold and to ask yourself, 'Is it actually the case that …?'

When Christian gathers data, he finds that his coworkers have not changed the way they act towards him. This disproves his basic assumption that speaking up would result in exclusion, and it improves his ability to stand up for himself and his needs.

Don't Try to Fix the Problem but Approach It with Curiosity

When you enter into complexity, not-knowing, confusion and conflict, your job is not necessarily to create clarity, knowing and harmony – to fix what does not work, sort out entrenched problems, make everybody happy.

It is possible not to understand what you discover and instead be confused about it and unsure how to deal with it. Rather than providing a solution, you have the option of asking curious questions, based on the belief that asking questions or saying things out loud can also help to open doors.

It can be tempting to react to mixed signals (like a coworker who says 'yes' while their body language says 'no' when you ask them to do something) by relying on the more convenient signal (the spoken 'yes') and ignoring the contradiction (the body language that says 'no'). However, it will be easier for you to engage with the mixed signals if you remind yourself that it is not your job to make the words and the body language align; your job is simply to be curious about what you notice.

> During a talk I was giving, a leader asked me, 'Should I go easier on myself? Sometimes I suppose I don't necessarily need to put on my executive hat?'
>
> This question leads to other questions: 'What does it mean for you to put on your executive hat?' and 'When does it feel so demanding to wear that hat that you feel the need to take it off in order to go easier on yourself?' And of course, 'Would it be possible for you to wear it AND go easier on yourself?'

The leader's question is based on an assumption that 'when I wear my executive hat, I need to be able to confront difficult issues and make them go away' (which is hard and heavy work), rather than being curious about the difficult issues and trust that putting it into words will make a difference and enable others to contribute to a solution (which is less hard and heavy work).

Stay with Everything That Is Present Here and Now

As part of my research project, I wrote the paper 'The struggle of staying with toxic emotions when all you want to do is leave' (2015). It is one thing to know what negative capability is and how it helps us and quite another thing to practise it, train it and stay with it.

Mindfulness offers both inspiration and specific methods, including practices that can help you stay with discomfort, as your resistance to discomfort and emotional pain gradually diminishes. Practices in which acceptance of and openness to whatever is present in the moment are central ingredients. The basic approach is not to strive towards any one goal in particular but to stay with what is. Not to judge, rate or evaluate (which we do much more than we generally realize because it plays such a prominent role in our context). Openly and patiently accepting what is and allowing it to be present, rather than trying to make it go away.

Hold Onto the Main Task

When you feel lost or lose your way among the many different emotions and potential directions you might take to navigate uncertainty, a helpful grounding practice may be to ask yourself 'What is the main task?' The main task for you and/or your group always guides what is relevant and what is not, so this question can help you prioritize if you feel overwhelmed by thoughts and feelings in the here-and-now.

Not-Knowing Is a Source of Curiosity

Because we are generally raised to think that *knowledge* is important, we may have a tendency to disqualify ourselves when we are not-knowing, just as we might worry that people around us will invalidate us. When we do that, we lose touch with ourselves, tell ourselves that we are not good enough and that we *ought* to know. By contrast, when we validate ourselves, we acknowledge not-knowing. Rather than seeing not-knowing as shameful or inadequate, not-knowing can be a potential source of learning.

Not-knowing is a source of creativity and enhanced curiosity. When you do not know, you can ask. When we think that we know, we typically do not ask questions. Negative capability goes hand in hand with learning. Training your negative capability includes putting energy into curious exploration rather than focusing on a quick and perfect solution.

Not-Knowing Helps You Move towards Empowerment

When you are not-knowing but curiously ask about your employees' ideas and experiences you move towards a more involving leadership style that helps your employees to see themselves as active cocreators of insights and knowledge rather than passive recipients who simply do what they are told.

Developing a Culture of Psychological Safety Does Not Require Knowing – On the Contrary

Psychological safety is about building a culture where everyone can share ideas, thoughts and emotions and take interpersonal risks without fear of negative consequences. When you train your negative capability and enhance your ability to stay with everything that is present in the room here and now (including complexity, confusion, different points of view and potential confrontations), you are also laying important foundation stones for a culture of psychological safety (more on this point in the discussion of Challenge 5).

TIPS

Use Whatever Imagery Works for You

I have a good colleague who – like me – is a winter swimmer. When she gets into the water, her strategy is to say to herself, 'Yes. It's cold – so what?' This helps her maintain calm breathing. I do the same every time I slip into the cold water. To me, this mindset has also proved helpful when I, metaphorically, step onto the creaking ice. 'Yes, it's creaking. So what? It is difficult because it's difficult. I am able to stay in it and with it.'

See Your Step as a Small Experiment

Begin by practising in less challenging situations that require some – but not too much – determination to stay with them. You can choose specific situations (a particular meeting or conversation, for example) or specific individuals (when you have an issue that is a little difficult to address) based on where you have most confidence that the ice will hold. This helps you enhance and build your tolerance to staying with the struggle, enabling you gradually to move into more challenging situations.

When you enter the difficulty and do not – immediately – know how to deal with it, see this step as a small experiment: What is your biggest fear? Are you worried about being invalidated by your coworkers, appearing incompetent or …? What actually happens when you do it? How do you feel in the situation? How do you feel afterwards? How do your coworkers perceive you?

Practise Tolerating All Sorts of Emotions

We are programmed to avoid difficult emotions. But ... difficult emotions are part of life.

Staying with the struggle is an indispensable part of mindfulness, because we instinctively step back whenever we encounter something that is difficult. However, if we focus and remain mindful, we can manage to stay with it. Mindfulness training helps us to embrace and stay with all sorts of emotions (see Challenge 2).

Training mindfulness means practising tolerating all sorts of emotions and remaining in a state of uncertainty. It is also an exercise in so-called receptive attending, which promotes a state of acceptance and activates our defences less.

Register Your Ability to Make Peace with Uncertainty and Discomfort

What is it like to be right here, right now? Seek out situations where you can do just that – and do it repeatedly. With repeated training, you will gradually enhance your psychological core and, thus, your capacity for making peace with uncertainty and discomfort (see Hougaard, 2016; Hougaard & Carter, 2022).

Resist the Urge to Rush to Action

Not-knowing is not incompetence – it is a platform for curiosity and engagement.

Stand by, stay with the difficulty and hold onto it. Take the time to notice what would be most helpful right now instead of wondering, 'What is the quickest way out of here?'

Say 'I Don't Know' When You Actually Do Not Know

Practise asking questions instead of thinking that you need to have all the answers. There is great power in this. A question that is not asked is a door that is not opened (see Adams, 2015).

Create Support Structures that Frame and Contain the Struggle

What will be helpful? What should you ask for? What should you work on to have it be present? What conversations should you invite in your group?

Build routines and structures for continually staying with what is and engaging in all sorts of conversations, the difficult as well as the energizing.

Working with capacities such as compassion, curiosity and humility in the group can provide a support structure for handling difficult situations.

Learn Skills That Feel Supportive When You Practise Your Negative Capability

Consider how it may help you to have a set of simple tools, such as skills related to conflict management, feedback, communication or other activities (read more in Challenge 4).

Note that skills and tools are means, not ends or solutions. Their effect depends on the situation, the relationships at play and how you use the skills or tools.

MY OWN PAGES

Essential to Me

What gets my attention?

What do I need to pay special attention to?

Micro-Acts I Want to Start With

What (small) step will I take?

When?

With whom?

What difference is it going to make (for me/the group/our mission)?

How will I know that I am succeeding (what will be/feel different in me/in the group/in relation to our mission)?

CHALLENGE

4

DOI: 10.4324/9781003582939-4

What do you think, Carolyn? Carolyyyyn??

How Do I Address Difficult Issues?

• Confrontation, conflict or different perspectives
• Fear of other people's opinions (FOPO)
• Avoid the sandwich model • Know your defences – always
• Caring candour • What? How? Who is in charge?
• No such thing as a free lunch • Direct, specific, factual
• Situation, behaviour, consequence • Clearing the snow as you go
• Disagreement commitment

Am I conflict-avoidant? Am I in the right frame of mind to confront it (sometimes it is easier to do it the next day if you are not having a great day)? How do I approach difficult issues without eliciting resistance and aggression (I don't want to shame anyone)? If I do this, will things get better – or what will the consequences be? Or the classic leadership dilemma: What if my (highly valued) employee gets angry if I address unacceptable behaviour, since I can't do without him/her? Isn't it better to leave the matter alone?

In working with elephants, these are frequently asked questions:

Most of us have tried circling around an issue, debating with ourselves whether we actually need to address it or whether it might just be okay or at least tolerable just to keep circling it.

DOI: 10.4324/9781003582939-4

The first question to be addressed is whether waiting for a better time is a case of mindful avoidance (see Challenge 2), or whether delaying will in fact be beneficial to yourself, others and your work performance.

Sometimes, an issue that feels difficult to address really *should* be addressed. It may be something that is difficult in the moment – here-and-now: When you would like to change the current situation you find yourself in.

What needs to be addressed may also be of a more general nature and related to your role as leader, such as an employee who should be relocated or moved to a different position, inadequate work performance or unacceptable behaviour in the workplace.

Often, when we need to address a difficult issue, we view the situation as a confrontation. As something that necessarily implies some form of conflict. Many would describe themselves as 'conflict-avoidant' because they recognize the tendency to circle around an issue. But why do we view it as conflict rather than seeing it as different viewpoints and perspectives and a sign of engagement? Why is it that different perspectives are expected inevitably to lead to conflict? Sometimes that is the case, but far from always. Perhaps we should also practise containing and actively using differences instead of mainly spotting and worrying about potential tension. In many cases, the core of the problem is that disagreements are not addressed in a timely manner and may therefore develop into conflict.

Thus, the challenge 'How do I address difficult issues?' contains several challenges in one.

One is the issue that was described under Challenge 3: What is it that makes it difficult for me to address difficult issues? What is it that I am afraid of? Challenges related to approaching the edge of our comfort zone also apply here. Addressing difficult issues can activate fundamental personal fears, such as the fear of rejection, of being seen as incompetent or of not being liked. It may also activate concerns over offending or upsetting others. One fundamental fear that is often activated is, 'What will others think of me?' Labels of being a people-pleaser and being conflict-avoidant often go hand in hand, since the desire to please everybody makes it difficult to say the things we assume they do not want to hear.

Another challenge has to do with getting better at addressing difficult issues in a way that is both empathetic and direct – both in the moment and in terms of the more general feedback style.

Finally, there is the challenge of helping to build a culture where it is easier to address difficult issues.

Let us examine the three constituent challenges one at a time.

CHALLENGE 4A: I AM A PEOPLE-PLEASER – WHAT DO I DO?

What do I do when I worry about what others will think of me? And whether they will like me?

POINTS FOR REFLECTION

FOPO

Michael Gervais, a psychologist specializing in high performance, is the author of an article in *Harvard Business Review* titled 'How to stop worrying about what other people think of you' (2019). His message is clear and precise: 'If you start paying less and less attention to what makes you *you* (...) and start conforming to what others may or *may not* think, you'll harm your potential.'

Michael Gervais's recommendations for conquering FOPO (fear of other people's opinions) involve cultivating greater self-awareness and developing a strong sense of who you are. In this effort to shift your focus from others' opinions to your own viewpoints, strengths and skills, it is essential to develop a personal philosophy.

Michael Gervais recommends reflecting on the following questions:

- When I'm at my best, what beliefs lie just beneath the surface of my thoughts and actions?
- Who are people who demonstrate characteristics and qualities that are in alignment with mine?
- What are those qualities?
- What are my favourite quotes? My favourite words?

The purpose of exploring these types of questions is to arrive at a clear sense of, 'Who am I? What do I stand for? How do I want to live my life?' That will help you maintain focus on what *you* are about rather than what others might think you ought to say or do.

Remember: Assumptions tend to become ingrained and spread from one context to another. That does not make them any more true, however, so you should always test them.

TIPS

Write Down Your Personal Philosophy

Who are you? What do you stand for? How do you want to live your life? Commit to acting in accordance with the principles of your philosophy. Start with people in your close network and then try to live out your principles in the workplace. When you encounter situations in which FOPO holds you back, simply acknowledge the fear and then reconnect to your philosophy (Gervais, 2019).

Define the People Who Matter to You

In his article, Gervais also refers to Brené Brown's book *Dare to Lead* (2018). In this book, Brené Brown – a scholar of vulnerability and leadership – suggests that you write the names of the people who matter to you on a card. The card should be no more than 3 x 3 centimetres, indicating that you need to be very selective and focus on the people whose opinions are truly important to you. Listen to their views and let the noise from all the other points of view fade into the background (Brown, 2018). This will help you be mindful in considering and choosing how you want to react to what (and to whom).

Test Your Assumptions (As Suggested in Challenge 3)

Often, our assumptions about what will happen and what others might think are not reflective of what will actually happen in the current situation. Especially not if we 'speak to the difficulty' based on decency and transparency (as I will describe later in this challenge).

CHALLENGE 4B: HOW DO I ADDRESS THE ISSUE?

How do I address the issue in a way that is clear; not too hard and not too soft; not too direct and not too vague?

POINTS FOR REFLECTION

Beware of the uncritical use of easily accessible tools.

When we are in doubt about how to approach something, our first step is often to call for help in the form of tools. What tools are available that might help us deal with the situation?

Tools are not a solution, but, as mentioned in the discussion of Challenge 3, it can be helpful to have a set of simple tools or models that can offer support when we need to address difficult issues. An important focus is to make sure the model does not take over, and that the feedback we offer is perceived as sincere and authentic. In one of the best-known and widely applied feedback models, the so-called sandwich model, this can prove a challenge.

The sandwich model involves first saying something positive, then addressing what should be changed or improved and then finishing off with another positive statement.

The assumption is that the middle 'layer' may be unpleasant to take in and should therefore be cushioned by the two positive 'layers'. However, the risk is that directness suffers and the positive statements ring hollow because the actual message is found in the middle statement.

In your search for an appropriate tool, you should ask yourself, 'What can help me say what I really want to say – in a way that is both direct and sensitive to the needs of the receiver?'

Again, Again, Again: Know Your Defences

In this situation too, it is important to know your own defences and the stories you tell yourself and to have an effective early warning system (see Challenges 2 and 3): What inner barriers get in the way of transparency and honesty? When do you begin to shirk the topic or cushion your statements excessively? What are the first signals telling you that you are now headed down the wrong path?

Are You a Storyteller, a Minimizer or a Speed-Talker?

The organizational consultants Henrik Adler and Emilie Sloth (2017) describe a number of defensive stereotypes to help you examine your own personal barriers in the form of common traps to fall into. Three of these stereotypes are:

- **The storyteller**: Provides explanations that are so lengthy, thorough and detailed that the points are lost, and the receiver will struggle to grasp both the essence and the seriousness of the feedback.
- **The minimizer**: Consistently minimizes the problem from the outset, so that the receiver struggles to understand why the feedback is offered, since the problem appears to be so minor.
- **The speed-talker**: Prefers to avoid the discomfort of the conversation and therefore delivers the message in a rushed manner without taking any real interest in the receiver.

Consider which of these stereotypes – or aspects of them – you recognize in yourself and thus need to be particularly mindful of?

Caring Candour: Direct Delivery with Caring Attention

Imagine two different working groups. In one group, people are super nice, caring and polite to each other. So polite and cautious, in fact, that they prefer not to share anything that might make anyone feel uncomfortable. They either avoid addressing difficult issues or cushion their statements excessively. In the other group, people are brutally honest and direct. Being straightforward is so important to them that they pay little attention to how their statements affect the receiver – even when the situation might appear both harsh and unpleasant.

Most people would prefer to avoid being a member of either group. An overly polite group is not a safe place to be because it lacks transparency, and people are in the dark about what the others are thinking. The highly confrontational group is also unsafe, and its members will typically try to keep a low profile, fly under the radar or do whatever they can to avoid becoming a target.

The challenge is to find the sweet spot in the middle: Caring candour.

Be Clear: What Is the Task? How Do We Do Things? Who Is in Charge of What?

Amy Gallo (2017), a writer and expert on workplace relations, distinguishes between four different workplace conflicts: Task, process, status and relationship conflicts.

- **Task** (disagreement over what the task or goal is)
- **Process** (disagreement over how to approach the task or achieve the goal)
- **Status** (disagreement over who is in charge of what)
- **Relationship** (personal disagreements, often involving difficult emotions such as anger and aggression)

If the first three types of conflicts are not addressed or resolved, there is a severe risk that they will develop into interpersonal conflicts. Hence, a key question may be, 'Is the group taking care to sort out any task, process or status issues to ensure clarity?' If your group has relationship conflicts, check if you agree on task, process and status issues, or whether there may be disagreements here that should be sorted out or resolved: what is the task, and what is the goal? How should the task be approached? Who is in charge of what?

No Such Thing as a Free Lunch

The organizational psychologist Birgitte Bonnerup (2024) describes the importance of trusting the process when you seek to resolve conflicts and processes that have become stuck. Trusting that it is possible to find a solution. She also underscores that conflict resolution always comes at a cost, since everyone involved has to be willing to give something up that might feel important: 'This may include values, habits or viewpoints or it may involve dismantling projections' (Bonnerup, 2024, p. 308). As you think about how to address an important but difficult issue, it may be important for you to consider, 'What am I willing to give up in order for us to find a solution and a path forward?'

TIPS

Check Your Communication

Check if your communication is assertive (clear and respectful) and steers clear of being submissive (being too quick to acquiesce to others' demands or requests) or aggressive (being harsh, critical and confrontational).

You are assertive when you are clear, acknowledge your own mistakes and contain others' mistakes.

The Basis of Your Feedback

Always check your intention behind providing the feedback you want to give: Who or what is supposed to benefit from the feedback? Make sure you make your point to the relevant individuals. This lets you be sure that you are not just getting something off your chest that does not really belong in the context where you address it. Who or what is going to benefit from your feedback – the task? The group? You?

Let the main task – your shared objective – guide your feedback. How does the behaviour you are addressing prevent you or the group from achieving your/its goal?

Be Specific and Factual

What are you seeing? What are you hearing? What are you noticing?

Be Direct

If you are being too wordy, you are typically cushioning your message too much. What is your point? How does the issue you are addressing hamper the group's performance?

As a Leader

Consider and address what is required for the employee to be successful.

As a Coworker

Consider and address what is required for us to accomplish our common goal.

Rely on a Structure

When offering general feedback, it can be helpful to rely on a structure. For example,

- What do you do that is helpful?
- What do you do that is less helpful?
- What would I like you to think about or do differently?

If you are instead providing here-and-now feedback on helpful or less helpful behaviour, address what is relevant in the situation. Avoid falling into the sandwich model trap, thinking that you necessarily have to find helpful behaviour to include in your feedback if the less helpful behaviour is in fact the essence of your message.

The 'Situation–Behaviour–Consequence' Model

One simple model you can use is the following:

> **Situation:** When we/you ...
> **Specific behaviour:** ... do/say ...
> **Consequence:** ... it makes me ... The consequence to me/us/the task is ...

The key point is to stick to specific, observable behaviour, so that the receiver understands your point and has a chance to change their behaviour. This is the opposite of using statements such as 'You are ... annoying, calculating, disruptive' and so forth, as these descriptions are both abstract (what do they actually mean?) and difficult to act on (what is the receiver supposed to do differently?).

Base Your Feedback on Your Own Experience

The 'situation – behaviour – consequence' model also helps you base your comments on your own experience: How YOU, in a specific situation, perceive a particular behaviour as less helpful because it has certain specific consequences.

Unlike opinions, experiences are not debatable. You can always stand by your experience. For example, in a disagreement, it makes a difference whether you say, 'That is not my experience' rather than 'I don't think that's how it is'/'You're wrong about that' and so on.

Perhaps you can feel how the former wording invites dialogue, while the latter invites discussion.

Clear the Snow as You Go

Make a habit of addressing all the little stones in your path to prevent them from piling up into major obstacles. Practise saying them out loud, the same way you say other things out loud. That can help make it just as easy and natural for Christian in the open-plan office to say, 'Would you mind keeping it down a little or stepping into one of the meeting rooms?' as it is to say, 'Would you bring an extra cup of coffee for me?'

CHALLENGE 4C: HOW DO WE BUILD A GROUP CULTURE WHERE DIFFICULT ISSUES ARE EASIER TO ADDRESS?

Perhaps you are familiar with the tiresome experience of being 'it' in a group. Or maybe you are familiar with the comfortable feeling of having a group member who is 'it': The one who is willing to stick their neck out and address difficult issues.

It may be important to make sure that responsibility for the group does not rest on just one person's shoulders. This can quickly turn into a habit that is both much too arduous for the person who is 'it' and much too enabling for the rest. It is crucial to build a culture that involves shared responsibility for addressing difficult issues.

Any culture is created by its members. Acts become habits, which become routines, which become culture. Thus, a culture consists of all the basic and taken-for-granted assumptions, including the ideas, opinions, taboos and so forth that hamper development.

Thus, to work with the group culture, it is relevant to consider the following points:

1. What are the basic assumptions we hold (and take for granted) that drive our behaviour and the way we interact with and relate to each other?
2. Our culture is shaped by everything we do. Behaviour becomes habits, which in turn become culture. What sort of things do we do that develop into (unchallenged) habits (without us even noticing)?

POINTS FOR REFLECTION

Examine the Basic Assumptions in Your Group that Stand in the Way of Your Goals

I once worked with a group that had some challenges when it came to giving each other feedback. They all wanted feedback but did not want to give it. Their leader thought they could use some help and invited a consultant to help the group develop good feedback practices. They were frustrated and annoyed with the consultant because they knew *how* to provide feedback – that was not the obstacle.

We then set out to uncover the underlying assumptions in the group culture: How come we do not provide feedback we know how it is done – and we would all like to receive feedback? What basic assumptions do we have that get in the way of addressing difficult issues?

One of the strong basic assumptions was, 'Who am I to tell him that? We're coworkers, after all.'

The process involved bringing this basic assumption to the surface and challenging it (what Chris Argyris (1974) refers to as double-loop learning) rather than training feedback techniques with the team (what Chris Argyris refers to as single-loop learning).

Promote Double-Loop Learning

Notice when the group you are part of turns to a quick and easy answer, as in 'this is how we solve that problem' (single-loop learning – more of the same), instead of examining the issue in depth: 'How come this is so hard for us?' (double-loop learning – more reflection, more critique, heightened awareness). This includes the question, 'What is it in our self-concept that prevents us from being effective?'

Taken-for-Granted Rules about What It Is Acceptable to Say

Carefully examine the basic assumptions you have in your group.

For example, are there basic assumptions that get in the way of you addressing difficult issues?

Amy Edmondson, professor of leadership, has carried out research that addresses typical taken-for-granted rules about when it is appropriate versus inappropriate to speak (she refers to these rules as 'implicit theories of voice').

Examples of these rules include,

- Don't criticize something the boss may have helped create.
- Don't speak unless you have solid data.
- Don't speak up if the boss's boss is present.

What You Do Shapes Your Culture, So Only Do Things that Promote What You Would Want to Be Part of

What sort of culture would you want to be part of/help build? How can you act in accordance with this? Are there any simple rules that would support the sort of culture you would want to be part of? For example, if you would like to be part of a mindful culture where people engage with each other, one simple rule could be, 'We switch off our phones and put them away during meetings.'

TIPS

A Contract Can Help the Group Along

A contract clarifies what the members of the group commit to doing and what they need others to commit to.

For example, a contract could include the following points:

- **A disagreement commitment**, meaning that the members commit to engage, also when disagreements arise, and to share their opinion if it differs from others'. It also marks a group intention of valuing disagreement and different perspectives as a way of promoting new, creative angles and ensuring that everyone has a voice and feels included.
- **Simple rules** that promote the sort of culture people would want to be part of. For example, phones are put away during meetings; everyone's voice should be heard when important decisions are made; conversations take place in the meeting rooms; and so forth.

Establish Structures that Help People Clear the Snow as They Go

For example, a helpful structure for summarizing meetings could include the following points: What am I glad we discussed? What did we not address which we need to table first thing, next time we meet? Also include a plan for check-ins/pit stops during the meeting: Is everybody on board? Are we on the right track? Are we focusing on the right topics?

What Comes Up at the Watercooler, in the Hallways or in the Car on the Way Home?

Help each other pick these perspectives or reflections up and decide where and how they should be addressed.

MY OWN PAGES

Essential to Me

What gets my attention?

What do I need to pay special attention to?

Micro-Acts I Want to Start With

What (small) step will I take?

When?

With whom?

What difference is it going to make (for me/the group/our mission)?

How will I know that I am succeeding (what will be/feel different in me/in the group/in relation to our mission)?

CHALLENGE 5

DOI: 10.4324/9781003582939-5

Is it just me, or does the atmosphere feel really tens-
Sshhh!

What Do I Do When There Is No Psychological Safety?

• Psychological safety is found outside the comfort zone.
• No shortcuts • What does the main task call for?
• If no one does anything … • Every drop counts
• Braintrust rules • Ask for help • Vulnerability and fallibility
• Structures that make things happen
• If only we talked more about … • Pit stops

When there is psychological safety, it feels okay to run interpersonal risks, to share concerns and ideas, to ask questions and to admit mistakes – without fearing the consequences.

Most of us want psychological safety. Most of us also want it *before* we step outside our comfort zone. In other words, we do not want to leave our comfort zone until we are sure that there is psychological safety. You might recall, 'It is better not to reveal how I feel; the group probably cannot handle it,' which is one of the significant plausible defensive stories we tell ourselves to avoid stepping out of our comfort zone. Paradoxically, however, by practising

DOI: 10.4324/9781003582939-5

avoidance behaviour, we are also contributing to a culture where people do not share how they feel, what they find difficult and so forth.

In *The Elephant in the Room* (2023), I refer to William Kahn (2001) professor of leadership and organizational psychology. His simple message is that in order to build trust, we have to act as if there is trust.

Thus, in order to build trust, we need to be willing to accept vulnerability by stepping outside our comfort zone. Trust does not develop automatically. We also need to make sure that we do not – consciously or unconsciously – try to remain in our comfort zone and make the path to psychological safety more accessible by lowering the bar for job performance. There are no shortcuts.

Job performance must always be part of the equation. Psychological safety is not an end in itself, since different tasks involve different needs for psychological safety. Thus, it is always helpful for you and your group to ask yourselves:

What does our main task call for? Where and why do we need greater psychological safety?

IF NO ONE DOES ANYTHING, NOTHING HAPPENS

In cultures characterized by apathy or anxiety, there is a significant risk that elephants are allowed to thrive and wreak havoc. Silence is the norm in situations that involve interpersonal risk.

At the same time, one challenge may be that small steps feel like a drop in the ocean: If you stick your neck out, will it even make a difference?

POINTS FOR REFLECTION

In Order to Build Trust, We Have to Act as if There Is Trust

Psychological safety does not develop automatically, and it is difficult to find while staying in our comfort zone. We cannot find safety unless we are willing to take a risk. In order to move towards a space where it is possible to take interpersonal risks, we must first be willing to take interpersonal risks.

When you manage to enhance your psychological safety, step by step, it also becomes easier to address issues that used to be difficult to address. This is simply because a culture built on the basic assumption that it is possible to share concerns and take interpersonal risks without fear of the consequences makes it more accessible to address difficult issues.

You Are Probably Not the Only Person Who Is Bothered by the Elephant

Another significant and plausible defensive stories we tell ourselves to avoid stepping outside our comfort zone is that 'It's probably just me.' In my research, I found that when one group member thinks, 'It's probably just me,' on average, two-thirds of the group members actually feel the same way. That should provide some food for thought.

Perhaps you have also experienced what a relief it is when someone else addresses something you have been thinking but were unable to say.

Every Drop Counts …

When you go out on a limb and take an interpersonal risk, it may feel as if 'there is a long way still to go.' But you have made a difference by taking a step that, hopefully, invites others to follow suit. It may feel like a drop in the ocean, but this is *your* contribution. You stuck your neck out and let yourself be seen. And that is Brené Brown's definition of courage (2018).

Psychological safety is not a phenomenon that is either present or absent. You can always help enhance the level of psychological safety. Rather than focusing on whether psychological safety is present or not, you should focus on your successes: Where and with whom do you experience psychological safety? Where and with whom could it be improved?

Establish Your Own Braintrust Rules

In her book *The Fearless Organization*, Amy Edmondson (2019) shares the following case story: After the success of *Toy Story* and during the work on *Toy Story 2* (which had gone off the rails), Pixar established what it calls its 'Braintrust' – a group of creative and experienced filmmakers and executives whose primary task is to improve stories and heighten the quality of Pixar's animated films with the goal of creating the best possible films. One of the basic rules of Braintrust is that all the members have to provide direct, honest and constructive feedback (caring candour, as described under Challenge 4).

The basic rules guiding the group's work are as follows:

1. Feedback must be constructive and must be about the project, not the person behind it. Similarly, the filmmaker must be ready to hear the truth and cannot be defensive or take criticism personally.
2. The feedback is suggestions – not prescriptions.
3. The feedback must come from a place of empathy – not from a fault-finding perspective.

What is your version of a Braintrust group? When do you need a Braintrust group? How can you create one? What rules do you need to help bring it to life?

TIPS

Statements to Enhance Psychological Safety

In *The Fearless Organization* (2019), Amy Edmondson suggests a set of simple but powerful statements to help you enhance the psychological safety of the rooms you find yourself in.

Simply practise saying the following:

- 'I don't know.'
- 'I need help.'
- 'I made a mistake.'
- 'I'm sorry.'

Each of these statements expresses vulnerability, and by expressing vulnerability and allowing yourself to be seen as fallible, you give others permission to do the same. Remember that if you are a leader and wish to move away from a zero-defects culture, you must be prepared and willing to share your own mistakes!

Amy Edmondson (2019) also proposes the following simple questions which you can use to reach out to others: Give it a shot. Look around you. Who could you invite into the learning zone with you?

Then ask,

- What can I do to help?
- What are you up against?
- What are your concerns?

Build Structures that Help Make It Happen

In Challenge 4, I suggest that you build support structures to ensure that you discuss difficult issues. In my workshops and elephant seminars, I often use sentence completion exercises, which can be helpful in certain situations.

Do a pit stop and ask everyone to complete the following sentences:

- 'I wish we would talk more about …'
- 'If we did, it would help us to …'

Share with each other and modify your contributions to ensure you talk about what is important for the individual group members, for the group as a whole and for the main task you are working on.

The following is a slightly more retrospective structure, which can help you develop transparency and make adjustments in the long term:

- 'I thought "If only I had said …" when …'
- 'But in the situation, I didn't, because …'
- 'Even though …'

This exercise can help you pick up signals that might have a slight lag (see Challenge 1), so that they can be brought back into the room, rather than remaining something that individuals take home or that is only brought up at the watercooler.

Curious Dialogue

You can also work with your sentence openings when you wish to invite curious dialogue (always make sure not to use them in a mechanical way!). A few examples:

- 'I wonder what ...'
- 'I am curious about ...'
- 'Tell me more about ...'
- 'Help me to understand how ...'

Curious Inquiries and Prompts

Similarly, you can use the following questions for curious inquiries and prompts[2]:

Do you feel that you are part of a culture where ...

- '... you can make mistakes without facing blame?'
- '... you are able to bring up problems and tough issues?'
- '... it feels safe to take a risk?'
- '... it is fairly easy to ask others for help?'
- '... your contributions are appreciated and put to use?'

How can you personally contribute to building such a culture?

When the Leader Wants to Build a Culture of Psychological Safety

In her *Harvard Business Review* article 'What is Psychological Safety?', Professor Amy Gallo (2023) offers four simple pieces of advice for leaders wishing to build a culture characterized by psychological safety:

1. Set the stage for inviting others' contributions: Explain why you need to hear from others, why their input matters and how it will impact the outcomes of the work.
2. Own up to your mistakes and share how you have learnt from them.
3. Actively invite input: What are you seeing? Where do you stand on this idea? What are your thoughts on this?
4. Replace blame with curiosity. Ask, 'What did you learn?'

The Power of Vulnerability

Watch Brené Brown's TED Talk 'The Power of Vulnerability' (2010), in which she shares insights and strategies for daring to be imperfect and building stronger relationships.

MY OWN PAGES

Essential to Me

What gets my attention?

What do I need to pay special attention to?

Micro-Acts I Want to Start With

What small step will I take?

When?

With whom?

What difference is it going to make (for me/the group/our mission)?

How will I know that I am succeeding (what will be/feel different in me/in the group/in relation to our mission)?

CHALLENGE 6

DOI: 10.4324/9781003582939-6

What Do I Do When Power Is Present in the Room?

• Power projections and fear of power
• Mindful alertness • Power as possibilities and space
• Integrity: What feels right? • 'No one was ever fired for keeping their mouth shut!'
• From watercooler to meeting table
• Authorize yourself • Leadership responsibility and shared responsibility
• Power-reflected communication
• Forget the enticing sandwich model

To many people, 'power' is a charged word. The associations are often negative, seen to reflect a worldview where the ends justify the means, and manipulation and backstabbing are part of the game. The politician Frank Underwood in the TV series *House of Cards* (2013–2018) is a perfect example of this perception, ruthlessly wielding his power with a kill-or-be-killed mindset. These common associations often contribute to a certain discomfort around power and powerful people.

People in positions of power are the targets of many projections. There are many fantasies and ideas about what people in powerful positions are like, what they think and how they act. Some of these ideas are reality-based and can

DOI: 10.4324/9781003582939-6

be underpinned with data. Others seem more imaginary, and supportive data seems hard to come by.

In this case, it is useful to ask yourself, 'What do I know, and what do I think?'

Formal Power

When we speak of power in organizations, we usually think of *formal power*, which is related to the formal leadership role.

Formal power may feel unpleasant, intimidating and frightening to employees since they are, of course, dependent on the leader. How will the leader's power be exercised in the case of disagreements or disputes? Will they be dismissed? Will they be demoted? Will they be out of consideration for new career possibilities? And so on and so forth.

We have all experienced how behaviours change when power enters the room. Personally, I recently took part in a leadership development programme that concluded with a lunch together with the powerful and high-profile CEO.

> The moment the CEO sat down at our table, the content and focus of the conversation changed. The main focus at the table went from 'celebrating a good and intense development process' to 'How can I put myself in the best possible light, so that the CEO will notice and appreciate me?'
>
> The consequence for everyone at the table was palpable. Suddenly, there was no more mutual attention or curiosity. However, the change also had a clear consequence for the CEO. He was cut off from taking part in the light and celebratory mood and the shared stories. Both the data he had access to and the atmosphere he experienced were very different, as the people around the table were highly selective about what data they now shared.

Mindful Alertness

In my research, I have come across a phenomenon that I call *mindful alertness*. It is a special form of attention that occurs when power is present in the room: A tiring and draining form of mindfulness characterized by readiness and alertness in relation to stakeholders with considerable authority or formal power. It is tiring because it involves a constant focus on playing your cards right. It is also a rather one-dimensional form of attention, as the focus is entirely on what is politically expedient, while everything else fades into the background.

While this is draining for the employee, it may be equally so for the leader, who needs and depends on their employees being transparent about the state of the organization. Where else is the leader going to get this information? This makes it harder for the leader to know and assess the true state of affairs for both employees and the organization.

Informal Power

In addition to the formal power embedded in the formal leadership role, there is the factor of *informal power* to consider: Power that people take or are given in their organization based on who they are or who they know:

- **Positional power**: What is your position in the organization?
- **Relational power**: Who do you know?
- **Personal power**: Who are you?

Informal networks of power play a key role in organizations in terms of implementing ideas and pursuing interests. Thus, to pursue an interest, it is important to have the strongest possible position based on three different types of power.

Interpersonal alliances are a way of controlling the informal organization. In pursuing a personal goal, joining forces is a source of power.

Power for All

Julie Battilana, professor at Harvard Business School and Harvard Kennedy School, and Tiziana Casciaro, professor at the Rotman School of Management in Toronto, have both studied the topic of power extensively and co-authored the book *Power, for All* (2021). As they present it, power is not the reserve of individuals in powerful roles. Instead, it is a necessary resource that can help us innovate, orchestrate change and make things happen that are important to us, our group and our shared task.

For example, if you are lacking a particular resource or piece of knowledge for your work, your task is to explore and identify who has or controls access to the things you need. Similarly, you possess informal power that you can use actively if you have access to resources that others need and value. This is an example of the deliberate use of power as a resource for seeing your ideas brought to fruition: A mindful strategy based on your particular sphere of influence.

In the deliberate use of informal power, ethics is always a key factor to ensure that you use your influence to make a positive difference for the group and the work effort you are part of (in contrast to the cut-throat use of power in which the ends justify the means, as mentioned in the introduction to this chapter).

An important reminder: Remember Søren from the opening section on theoretical cornerstones – the group member who is trying to increase his own sense of power by getting closer to someone he views as powerful? This is about something else. This is *not* a deliberate – mindful and ethical – strategy but an unconscious avoidance strategy driven by defence.

Thus, the challenge 'What do I do when power is present in the room?' contains several challenges in one:

1. First of all, there is the challenge of getting better at seeing – and constructively using – power games and political dynamics in complex and nontransparent organizations.
2. Second, there is the challenge of finding the best way to bring up elephants with the boss.
3. And finally, the leader faces the challenge of being aware of the significance of their power when they bring up elephants with their employees.

Let us look at the three challenges one at a time.

CHALLENGE 6A: HOW CAN I GET BETTER AT SEEING – AND CONSTRUCTIVELY USING – POWER IN COMPLEX AND NONTRANSPARENT ORGANIZATIONS?

Alliances and informal networks can be difficult to spot. Near invisible. It does not help that people often say one thing and do another.

So, how can I learn to spot power games and political dynamics? How can I be mindful of them? Noticing when they are active? And how can I be more mindful of what is going on when I am part of them myself?

And how do I avoid automatically practising mindful alertness, simply manoeuvring to be close to power and saying what I think the person in power wants to hear without considering what I think is right or wrong? How do I avoid losing myself in power games and political dynamics?

POINTS FOR REFLECTION

Power is Also about Resources and Possibilities

Do you mainly view power as a despicable and manipulative phenomenon? Or could you view power as an opportunity and as a chance for your interests to be realized? Might you view power as something that could help achieve what you need – what is important for you to influence or accomplish?

If you begin to examine power as an opportunity, this may open some doors and enable possibilities that you can begin to explore: Who can help you gain access to what you appreciate and need in order to achieve what is important to you?

Understanding where the power is found can be a way to understand what is going on in your organization and who can help by providing key resources.

Positions of Power Attract Projections

Examine your own projections in relation to positions of power: What do you know and what do you think? What is imagined and what is reality?

Often, it can be helpful to review your previous experiences with people in power:

> What experiences do you carry with you and (unfairly) project on people who are in positions of power in your current organization? How do your experiences keep you from speaking to what is important to you, your group or your shared work task? How can you challenge the past experiences you bring into the current situation?

Mindful Alertness and Lack of Transparency Are Key Sources of Stress

In many ways, my research underscores the importance of transparency in organizations. Not just in terms of clarifying tasks and responsibilities but also at a relational level: Whom can I rely on? Will people tell me the truth? Am I getting clear and direct feedback?

In terms of stress and well-being, my research shows that the primary threat is *not* too many tasks or too little time. Instead, the primary threat is a lack of transparency. One of the most stressful states we can be in is the state of mindful alertness. Alertness requires a huge effort and a lot of energy. The source of stress is that so much energy is expended on determining 'What do others need from me?' and 'Is what I'm doing good enough?', rather than focusing on 'What do I need in order to deliver a good work effort?'

Notice whether you practise mindful alertness yourself. If so, in relation to whom, and what are the consequences?

TIPS

Ask Generous Questions about Group Dynamics

The ability to read and understand others is generally crucial, so be curious about group dynamics and be generous with questions such as these:

- What might be happening here?
- What is driving this decision?
- What are we gaining?
- What are we avoiding?

Observe and Pay Attention to Decision-Making Processes

How are decisions made? Who is involved? What voices are heard and taken seriously? What voices are not heard and taken seriously? Are some voices systematically excluded – and what are the potential consequences of that?

You can let in any voices that are not heard – but which provide important messages – by enquiring about them with curiosity. You can also share your observation and your assessment of the consequences.

Use Emotions as Data

Emotions can help you access information about what might be going on, so train your ability to use them. Emotions can guide the questions you explore with your group (as described in Theoretical Cornerstones).

Listen, Be Curious and Reach Out

Listen to other people's perspectives and experiences; be curious and reach out to people who might help you access the resources you need.

Act with Integrity

When you reach out to the people who control your access to what you appreciate, notice whether you feel true to yourself and what you stand for, or whether you feel that you are taking a step away from yourself. That can be a good ethical guide to ensure that you are acting with integrity. It is easy to be sucked into power games and political agendas without really noticing it. So check in with yourself: What feels right?

Rock the Boat

In *The Elephant in the Room*, I refer to Professor Debra Meyerson's book *Tempered Radicals: How Everyday Leaders Inspire Change at Work* (2003). Meyerson addresses the delicate balance involved in wanting to be part of a community while staying true to yourself.

In order to act with integrity, you need to make sure that what you stand for does not challenge existing norms and routines head-on, as that can make it difficult for people to take in your views. Meyerson uses this helpful image: Rock the boat but not so hard that you fall out of it. Or so hard that others go overboard. But still: rock the boat – and keep rocking it!

CHALLENGE 6B: HOW DO I BRING UP ELEPHANTS WITH MY MANAGER?

Knowing what you can and cannot bring up when power is present in the room can be a challenge in itself. A powerful person who has the right to hire and dismiss employees can have a strong influence on what seems possible and legitimate to discuss.

How do you bring up elephants when the leader is in the room? The leader might disagree with your point of view and may get angry or annoyed (perhaps because they ought to have brought up the elephant themselves, or because they are part of the elephant ...), may reduce your bonus or turn down your request for a course you really wanted to attend ... Or maybe you heard stories of previous incidents, such as 'When a coworker spoke up, he was let go within six months.'

Amy Edmondson gives a very precise description of how our instinctive urge to tread with caution and avoid interpersonal risks spontaneously kicks in when power is involved

(2019). This makes it easy to err on the side of caution, thinking 'No one was ever dismissed for keeping their mouth shut' and keeping a low profile by letting risk avoidance govern what we do and say.

POINTS FOR REFLECTION

Your Projections on the Leader's Role Are Not Necessarily Apt for Your Current Leader

As part of my research design, I had my informants make drawings. In situations characterized by mindful alertness, individuals with power generally played a prominent role in the drawings: They were much larger than other people in the drawings. This was not always the result of a conscious choice, as in 'I'm enlarging my supervisor, because he is the leader.' Instead, it was rather a reflection of the person's unconscious projections and fantasies about the leadership role – translated into a large figure in the drawing. In relation to this, an important question for further exploration is: 'What do you actually know about the person who is in the leadership role – and what are your projections on persons in positions of power?'

This may be the first important question to ask yourself. As part of this, you can also explore whether, for example, thinking 'I won't say anything; if I do, she'll just cut my training course' might be an example of mindful avoidance – a story you tell yourself in order to stay inside your comfort zone (see Challenge 2).

Your Manager Depends on You to Tell the Truth

A few years ago, I attended a conference when a member of the leadership team in a large IT company was asked, 'If you could only do one thing in leadership, what is the one thing that would make a major difference?'

His reply was, 'If you could move all the watercooler conversations in our organizations into the meeting rooms, where the messages need to be delivered, THAT would make a big difference.'

Recently, I visited an organization where the top leadership sometimes asked the canteen staff what people talked about at the watercooler.

The higher your position in the organizational hierarchy, the more you depend on your employees to tell you the truth. How else can you know what is happening in your organization? Often, there is a reason why the watercooler talk is not brought up in meetings: It is associated with interpersonal risk. However, watercooler conversations contain obvious data for curious inquiry: What do we talk about in this informal context? And why is it difficult to bring up in a more appropriate setting?

This mindful focus can prevent a culture where all the risky issues are avoided and swept into the corners.

Authorize Yourself as a Valid Source

Am I really a valid source of feedback to my leadership? Will they listen to me, or will they see it as inappropriate for me to share what I experience? In short: Can I authorize myself to share what is important to me when there is an authority in the room?

All these questions depend on context – meaning that they depend on the culture that has been created, including which topics are allowed and which are off-limits. In this context, of course, you need to consider how best to be heard in the context you are part of. Therefore, the main question you should ask yourself is, does my experience/feedback matter for whether and/or how our cooperation and joint work effort will succeed? If your answer is 'yes', can you use that to authorize yourself and find your voice?

Some Things Are the Responsibility of Leadership – Some Things Are Your Responsibility

'But that's the responsibility of leadership!' I often hear that from employees who, for one reason or another, have become tired of trying or have given up. Often for good reason. As always, it is crucial to examine this statement carefully for indications of potential mindful avoidance: What is real, and what might be unhelpful avoidance behaviour?

Yes, leadership has a special responsibility and role. No, employees should not take on any formal leadership responsibility. However, everyone has a shared responsibility for enabling conditions that are important for themselves, the group and the shared work task.

So ask yourself, 'What sort of culture do I want to help create, and what is my sphere of influence?'

TIPS

Practise Small Helpful Steps

Ask a question, share a thought, share an observation, share an emotion.

Pay Attention to Whether You Are Practising Mindful Alertness

Are you concerned about the consequences of addressing something that is important to you, your group, your work task? Consider what the consequences will be of *not* addressing it.

Be Clear About Your Message

Make sure not just to provide the answers that leadership wants to hear – and watch out for signals which tell you that you are at risk of doing just that. It may be helpful for you to prepare and be clear about your message by asking yourself, 'What is the most important point I want to make?'

It can also be helpful to prepare how you want to initiate a conversation about the most important issue to bring up, for example:

- 'For the sake of clarity, I would like to share my experience of ...'
- 'Before we make a decision on xx, it would be helpful if you would take a moment to listen to an experience from my area ...'

Base Your Contribution on Your Experiences Rather Than Your Points of View

Points of view are debatable and may, therefore, invite discussion. Experiences are not debatable (no one can cancel or disagree with the experience you had) and are, therefore, more suited to inviting dialogue.

Doubt Indicates a Need for Greater Transparency

If you are in doubt about which topics are allowed and which can be addressed when the leadership is present in the room, this indicates a need for greater transparency.

So are you able to ask questions? Are you able to share your doubts? For example, by asking questions such as,

- 'There is a challenge concerning xx, which I need to discuss with you. Is this something we can discuss in this forum, or is there another time when it would be more appropriate?'

- 'What decisions have been made, and where would it be helpful for you to have our input?'

Draw Up a Social Contract

You can help each other at the watercoolers when issues come up that would be helpful to bring up in a meeting. You can do that by drawing up a social contract, agreeing that when this happens, you will ask each other the following questions:

- 'How do we address it?'
- 'When do we address it?'
- 'Who should we involve?'

Base Your Contribution on Your Sphere of Influence, and Be Transparent

When you think that something is the responsibility of leadership and calls for action from leadership, base your contribution on your sphere of influence and be transparent in relation to leadership:

What do the leaders need to do? What are they not hearing or seeing that is important for the execution of the main task? What are the consequences?

You may even have suggestions as to what might be needed.

CHALLENGE 6C: AS A LEADER, HOW CAN I BE MINDFUL OF THE IMPACT OF MY POWER WHEN I BRING UP ELEPHANTS WITH MY EMPLOYEES?

Leaders must remain mindful and reflective with regard to the significance of their power. As described in previous sections, a formal position of power will always lead to mindful alertness and avoidance. That is one important point for the leader to be mindful of. The related challenge is to display behaviours and build structures that counteract both avoidance and alertness.

Furthermore, the leader's words will always carry special weight because they come from a position of power. This is another important point for the leader to be mindful of. The related challenge is to engage in communication that is based on a reflective understanding of power.

POINTS FOR REFLECTION

Be Open about Leadership and Decision-Making Processes

A key factor in relation to transparency is the need to be open about leadership and decision-making processes. This makes power relations clear and easy to navigate, compared to when they are hidden. Remember that, for your employees, the leadership space is a projective space. This means that it is part of your job to help give your employees access to real data rather than leaving it up to their imagination.

You Hold Formal Power: Therefore, Everything You Do Should Be Based on a Reflective Understanding of Power

The book *Feedback Gentænkt* [Feedback Rethought] (Trillingsgaard, 2017) includes a chapter by the organizational psychologists Morten Fogsgaard and Maiken Rønde Olesen on the concept of feedback that is based on a reflective understanding of power. In it, they underscore that leaders and employees are not equals in the organizational hierarchy. This means that there are limits to what people can say.

In this context, the traditional feedback models – including the widely used sandwich model (first you say something positive, then you explain what needs to be improved, and then you make another positive statement) – are seductive because they offer a simple structure that sometimes allows us to avoid a difficult topic. However, they are also dangerous because the actual message may end up being so cushioned that it becomes difficult to hear it.

Thus, the leader has a special responsibility to be specific and direct to avoid opening the door to speculation and worries for the employee, such as 'I wonder what he is going to bring up next?' or 'What was his point?'

In feedback that is based on a reflective understanding of power, it is important to be clear about 'What is the situation?' (What am I seeing, hearing, noticing?), and 'What are the consequences?' (this affects/influences …). The leader also needs to remember to help the employee move forward, for example by asking, 'What is the next step?' and 'What do you need from me?'

TIPS

Be Clear

It is essential that the formal authority is clearly defined and that you are clear about your role and responsibility. By acknowledging and addressing the power you hold, you can prevent it from operating under the surface. You can do that, for example, by being clear about the following aspects:

- What decisions have been made? How much room is there for influence and involvement?
- Where do we have shared interests, and where do our interests diverge?

Set the Stage

Because there is a fairly high likelihood that people will feel less free to speak their minds when the leader is present in the room, it is crucial that you set the stage to invite your employees to provide input:

> What is the task, what are the conditions, what is possible, and what is not possible? What do you need to hear from your employees? Why is it important? And how does it affect the outcomes of your joint work?

'Setting the stage' has a containing effect and contributes to a culture of psychological safety (as described in Challenge 5).

Invite Input

When you have made the possibilities of influence and involvement clear, *actively invite input* from your employees:

> What are you seeing? Where do you stand on this? What are you thinking?

To ensure maximal transparency – and to get all the potential input – you may do one more round before you wrap it up:

> 'Okay. It's important to get all the input you can provide. So I want to ask if there is anything that you are seeing or thinking that might feel difficult to share but which is important for the topic at hand. Think about for a minute and let me know.'

MY OWN PAGES

Essential to Me

What gets my attention?

What do I need to pay special attention to?

Micro-Acts I Want to Start With

What (small) step will I take?

When?

With whom?

What difference is it going to make (for me/the group/our mission)?

How will I know that I am succeeding (what will be/feel different in me/in the group/in relation to our mission)?

CHALLENGE

7

DOI: 10.4324/9781003582939-7

I hope you understand that...!
...because I can't explain...

How Do I Deal with Impression Management and Pretence?

• *Positive impression management* • *Pretence*
• *A question of authenticity* • *The flipside of impression management*
• *The fear of being found out* • *Myths of vulnerability*
• *Healthy or unhealthy compromise?*

Most of us have probably experienced the difference between frontstage and backstage – terms that were first introduced by the sociologist Erving Goffman. There is a difference between what is said in the restaurant kitchen and what is said in front of the diners. Between what is said in internal meetings and what is said in client meetings. Naturally. This difference makes good sense because tasks and roles differ between the two contexts.

When we are frontstage, we will often be focused on creating a particular impression or painting a particular picture of ourselves because we would like others to perceive us in a particular way. This is often referred to as 'impression management'.

It is natural to be especially attentive, try to make a good impression and do an extra stellar job in front of the boss or

DOI: 10.4324/9781003582939-7

an important client. In many companies, for example, there is a noticeable difference in dress code based on whether people are going to spend the day at the office or whether they are going to meet with a client. Making an extra effort and trying to put your best foot forward is *not* the same as being less authentic. It is simply a way of highlighting certain aspects of ourselves and making a special effort.

It only becomes a problem if it tips over, and the effort to fashion a particular impression becomes an unconscious and draining routine. Constant frontstage work is hard. It can intensify mindful alertness (as discussed under Challenge 6), the constant effort to calculate how to look our best to certain individuals.

The sociologist and media scholar Joshua Meyrowitz (1985) introduced the term *forward frontstage*, an expanded frontstage concept that involves an even greater emphasis on impression management by only ever presenting the nice, polished, politically correct version of oneself and playing all the cards right.

One of my former tutors at the University of Copenhagen, Professor of Psychology Martin Johansen, once described the phenomenon of pretence in a lecture. I clearly remember the experience he described and how it affected him: His parents were having some people over for dinner, the stress level in the kitchen was high, and his mother had just had a row with his father. The mood was intense and unpleasant until the doorbell rang, and his mother opened the door to greet the guests with a big smile and a warm 'Welcome!' The young boy was confused and could not make sense of what he was seeing: How could his mother suddenly be so cheerful?

This brings us to the flipside of mindful alertness. In a culture of mindful alertness, it is crucial to be able to influence or even control the impression we make on others: We carefully select what we wish to share with others and what to hide. We strive to maintain a carefully fashioned self-image – at all costs.

This presents an obvious challenge. If an organization generally has a strong frontstage culture, where impression management has an important impact on interactions in the work process, the result is a non-transparent culture.

In such a culture, there will be many questions about authenticity: What is actually real and sincere? Impression management appears in its purest form in social media, where it is possible to choose the exact filter to apply to the real and original expression.

To the individual, this is all exceedingly exhausting. Both because the impression we would like to present to the outside world does not always match who we really are or how we feel and because we are striving to control something that is outside our sphere of influence, namely other people's perceptions and experiences.

The effort to try to control other people's perceptions of us is often accompanied by a fear of being found out: What if they discover who I really am, what I am actually capable of and where my limitations are?

This draws so much energy that other relationships – which can be characterized as being more genuine – slip into the background. It is also obvious that intense impression management gets in the way of building a culture of psychological safety, where having the courage to own up to our shortcomings and sharing our mistakes is an essential quality of a high-performing team.

Cultures that tip over into excessive impression management also have a tendency to buy into the myths of vulnerability that Brené Brown (2012) has addressed in her research:

Myth no. 1: Vulnerability is weakness.
Myte no. 2: I don't do vulnerability.
Myth no. 3: Vulnerability is letting it all hang out.
Myth no. 4: We can go it alone.

Buying into the myth that showing vulnerability equals weakness, which should be avoided, presents an obstacle to a courageous culture, because all micro-acts will involve a high degree of masking, as potential vulnerabilities are covered up or pushed aside.

HOW DO I AVOID GETTING CAUGHT UP IN PRETEND PLAY?

Knowing when positive and helpful impression management tips over into inauthentic and non-transparent pretend play is a critically important factor. It is crucial to be able to recognize this both in ourselves and in others.

POINTS FOR REFLECTION

Practise Being Honest and Providing Sincere and Reflective Input

In cultures with a high degree of impression management and mindful alertness (Who is present in the room that I need to impress or look good to?), you can find inspiration in the moderately radical approach of speaking your mind in a way that gives you a chance of being heard. Rock the boat, but not so much that you fall out of it.

Practise staying true to yourself and providing sincere input while considering the context you find yourself in.

Identify Your Own Personal Warning Signals Indicating Insincere Compromises

Just as you need to know your own personal warning signals in relation to mindful avoidance, you also need to know and notice the warning signals that tell you that your impression management is beginning to tip over into mindful alertness. What are the first indications that you are beginning to compromise yourself, your values and your goals? Is it a healthy compromise in which you let others know where you stand while also expressing your willingness to compromise (for the sake of the work task), or is it an unhealthy compromise, in which you pretend to agree because you do not want to draw negative attention to yourself or risk looking less good to important others?

Be Curious about What Actually Drives Your Behaviour

Be curious about what drives your behaviour: Why am I actually doing this? What do I gain and what do I lose? What am I avoiding – and why?

TIPS

Alleviate Confusion with Curiosity

Be curious and ask when you are confused about the signals you are picking up.

When in Doubt – Ask

When you are unsure whether you are compromising yourself, ask yourself,

- Is what I am doing now helpful in relation to our shared task?
- Is there a basis for a genuine and meaningful relationship?

MY OWN PAGES

Essential to Me

What gets my attention?

What do I need to pay special attention to?

Micro-Acts I Want to Start With

What (small) step will I take?

When?

With whom?

What difference is it going to make (for me/the group/our mission)?

How will I know that I am succeeding (what will be/feel different in me/in the group/in relation to our mission)?

CHALLENGE 8

DOI: 10.4324/9781003582939-8

What Do I Do if I Have Become the Designated Elephant Handler?

• Valency • Give up the rewards • Pass the work back to the group • The responsibility is always shared • Lower the bar • Stay with yourself • Invite others in

Many groups develop a phenomenon where one person is generally assigned the responsibility of dealing with elephants: One person whom the other group members can always rely on to bring up any difficult issues, speak up and engage in confrontations.

Always having that role can be very hard work. Another drawback is that the group becomes dependent on having this one person speak on behalf of the group. If it is not clear that an individual is speaking on behalf of the group, another risk is that the presented viewpoints are attributed to the spokesperson alone. Thus, instead of appearing as a group phenomenon, the input risks becoming

DOI: 10.4324/9781003582939-8

individualized and attributed to the speaker: 'Well, you know, Matt is always ...'

In this situation, it is important for the individual not to feel solely responsible for the group dynamic. Similarly, it is important for the group not to make the individual responsible, but to work as a group in addressing the issues that are important for the execution of the group's main task.

Under Theoretical Cornerstones, I briefly discussed the psychological concept of having valence for a particular role. In this context, the role is being the person who always brings up the elephant.

Valence describes what we are inclined to do and our tendency to take on the sort of role that matches our inner needs. This may be a need to be the cool person who can handle any situation. The brave person who is not afraid to speak their mind. The heroic person who never hesitates to stand up for the group. The responsible person who picks up the slack.

If you have valence for always taking responsibility, you will be mobilized in a group where other members try to shirk their responsibilities. Often, this is not a conscious choice, but as with many other kinds of automatic behaviour, you can enhance your awareness of your own valences and learn to recognize them when they are not helpful.

Even when the roles you have valence for seem draining, they may still be associated with perceived rewards. For example, it may be tiring to take on the role of the responsible person if it means picking up the slack for others, but it may hold rewards, for example in the form of perceived control or a feeling of superiority. Thus, when you would like to escape the burden of a particular role, you also have to be prepared to give up the rewards.

AS A GROUP, HOW DO WE MAKE SURE EVERYONE TAKES RESPONSIBILITY FOR THE ELEPHANTS? HOW CAN THE INDIVIDUAL GROUP MEMBER GIVE UP HOLDING SOLE RESPONSIBILITY – AND HOW CAN THE GROUP TAKE ON ITS SHARE OF THE RESPONSIBILITY?

Creating a culture where it is okay to talk about the elephants is always a shared responsibility. The initiative often comes from individuals who (as described under Challenge 2) begin to challenge existing norms and behaviour patterns – precisely because all change begins with micro-acts within people's own sphere of influence. It is, however, important to make sure that the initiator does not simply do the work on behalf of the group, allowing the other group members to deposit the difficult work with the member who has valence for picking it up.

POINTS FOR REFLECTION

Be Ready to Give Up the Rewards of the Role You Have Taken on

What are your valences, and what rewards do they bring? Consider where it might be tipping over, so that you end up doing the group's work: When do you end up doing other group members' work or picking up slack when you wish that others would pitch in?

Pass Whatever You Pick Up Back to the Group

How can you pass the work back to the group, rather than doing the work for them? Instead of speaking for others, could you ask other questions that address what you have picked up, rather than simply assuming responsibility for it yourself?

If you asked the question, you have done enough.

The Key Is Not to Switch to the Other Extreme

'I'll keep my mouth shut because normally, I'm always the one who speaks up.' The solution is not to abandon the responsibility entirely and shut down (attempting indifference). The solution is to strike the right balance so you can give up some of the elephant work you end up doing and instead aim (simply) to put it on the table, saying, 'This is the elephant I am seeing. What are we going to do about it?'

TIPS

Lower Your Ambitions, Lower the Bar

Notice when responsibility tips over into excessive responsibility by registering how you feel when you go forward. If you are filled with irritation, anger, frustration, fatigue and powerlessness and a sense of injustice, these are indications that you are moving into the territory of excessive responsibility. These are all signals telling you to lower the bar.

Pay attention to your own signals – and a little less to what others might wish, expect or need you to do.

Practise Staying with Yourself

Continually practice staying with yourself instead of seeping into others.

What do you need to say that would help you – simply – to be content with your own contributions rather than getting frustrated over others'?

Invite Others In

Over and over again.

MY OWN PAGES

Essential to Me

What gets my attention?

What do I need to pay special attention to?

Micro-Acts I Want to Start With

What (small) step will I take?

When?

With whom?

What difference is it going to make (for me/the group/our mission)?

How will I know that I am succeeding (what will be/feel different in me/in the group/in relation to our mission)?

CHALLENGE 9

DOI: 10.4324/9781003582939-9

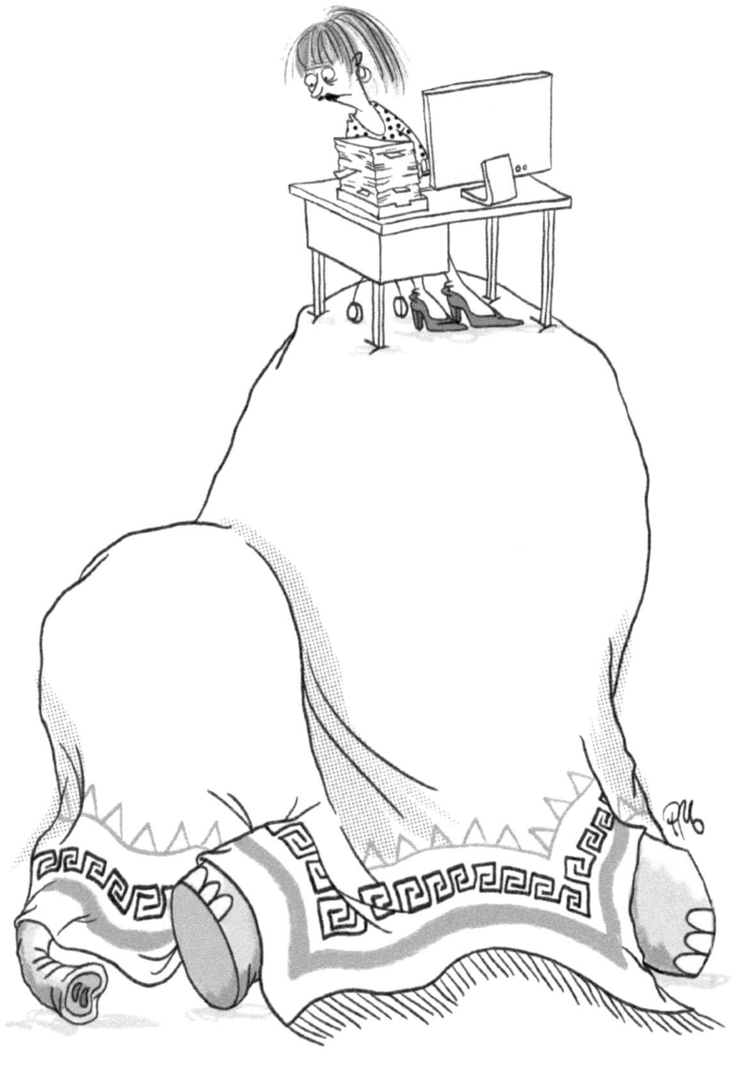

How Do I Approach the Big Elephants That Have Been Around for Much Too Long?

• Broaching the issue ... • The overinflated balloon • Something to be 'fixed' • Micro-acts add up • The elephant's ecosystem • Trust the process • Evaluated in your sphere of influence

Some of the elephants that may feel toughest to discuss are the ones that have been allowed to live their own lives. Often, they have been allowed to exist for much too long.

There are many small examples of these kinds of elephants:

- An employee who has been allowed to disparage coworkers and spread fear because this particular coworker is professionally competent, and the leadership lacks the courage to set boundaries for fear that this valued employee might quit.

DOI: 10.4324/9781003582939-9

- A coworker who always shirks their share of the responsibility. This behaviour may have begun in minor ways, based on plausible rationalizations. After gradually expanding, it has now become a source of frustration.

What typically feels difficult is broaching the issue because the problematic behaviour has now become a pattern and an established norm. When something 'should have been done a long time ago', it can feel especially hard to find the right time and the right way to address the problematic behaviour. Once the right moment has passed, the timing rarely feels very good. This is what makes the stories we tell ourselves about why 'we may as well wait and see' so compelling.

CHALLENGE 9A: WHEN DO I ACT? WHAT IS THE BEST TIMING WHEN THE MOMENT IS LONG OVERDUE?

Often, the main challenge in relation to elephants that have been around for a long time is the question, 'Why now?' and, once it has been decided that action is overdue, 'What is the best timing?'

The challenge of timing for bringing up old elephants is usually related to the notion that *now* it is time to fix or eliminate the elephant and that bringing up the elephant is the same as exposing it *completely* and getting rid of it *for good*.

This is often viewed as confronting a longstanding source of frustration – like a balloon that has become overinflated and is now close to popping. This is often the feeling that drives the decision finally to take action. Consider the following:

Is the question of timing really the most important question?

First Thought: Do I View it as Something I Need to Sort Out on My Own?

To many leaders, this becomes a question of finding the right time for a difficult confrontational conversation aimed at 'dealing with' the elephant. Especially if you have a leadership role, many will expect it to be your responsibility to 'deal with the elephant'.

Ultimately, that may well be the case, but still, you may be placing too heavy a burden on your own shoulders. What would it be like if you instead thought of the elephant as an issue that should be gradually exposed – step by step and in the midst of it all? A creature that should no longer be allowed to walk around undisturbed but which should gradually be made the subject of examination and engagement? What would happen if the question of timing were reframed as a question of mindfulness in the moment? How can you begin to be mindful of – and address – the elephant step by step? If you approach it this way, the timing is *now*! Continually! All the time! Step by step ...

To begin to poke the elephant is the same as signalling, 'I see you, you're not supposed to be here, it is not okay.' Once the elephant is gradually made the subject of examination, and if, for example, the need for a one-on-one conversation becomes clear, probably the right timing for this conversation is likely to become clear.

Next Thought: Do I View This Act as a Confrontation?

If you recognize the sensation of a balloon that is about to pop when you look at a big elephant, it is important to take a step back so you can address this difficult issue from another vantage point than 'overinflated balloon'.

It is never too late to begin to address an issue and thus avoid letting the unsaid pile up until it is suddenly put on the table all at once. Think of the problematic behaviour as something you are now going to begin to address. Broach the issue by bringing up new and fresh examples, rather than pulling all the dusty old incidents out of storage. Draw inspiration from the tips for addressing difficult issues that are described under Challenge 4.

TIPS

Explore What Behaviours Add Up to Become an Elephant

What individual micro-acts constitute the larger challenge that has become something everyone gives a wide berth? How can you begin to address these micro-acts? In the moment, while they are happening – or immediately after they occurred?

At a more general level, explore the following issues:

- What are your most common avoidance strategies? (See Challenge 2)
- In which situations do you typically fail to address what should be addressed in the moment?
- How and with whom can you begin to address what should be addressed, being especially mindful of the elephant you are seeking to diminish?

CHALLENGE 9B: WHAT ABOUT THE ELEPHANT'S ECOSYSTEM? WHAT DO I DO ABOUT THAT?

The challenge is not just the elephant in itself but also all the avoidance routines that have co-existed with the elephant for a long time. Thus, the avoidance routines and the ecosystem surrounding the elephant also need to be addressed. After all, the elephant fed on something. It was part of a system that allowed it to grow bigger and stronger. This makes it important to consider the factors that enabled the elephant: What did we all contribute to create the conditions that allowed the elephant to thrive?

It is essential to approach this as a joint responsibility and to examine the structures, norms, routines and so forth that enabled the elephant in the room to continue to grow.

POINTS FOR REFLECTION

Approach This as a Joint Responsibility and Establish Support Structures

It is important to examine the group's behaviour and norms. What is it that enables elephants to thrive and grow? In this effort, it can be helpful to consider what support structures (see Challenge 5) might be helpful to establish in the group to ensure that you are able to address unhelpful practices continually and step by step.

Take Micro-Acts Seriously

Might there be a tendency to dismiss micro-acts, saying, 'It's no big deal.' If that is the case, this presents an important factor to focus on, as it may contribute to things piling up.

Micro-acts that do not contribute to the desired culture, promote well-being and facilitating the efficient execution of the main task should always be the subject of curious inquiry.

TIPS

Examine Your Meeting Structures and Shared Time

How do you spend time together? And how do you make room for discussing unhelpful factors and celebrating and enhancing the helpful ones? Might there be a tendency for Task 1 (our joint task) to draw so much focus that Task 2 (how we work together to achieve our joint task) slips too far into the background?

Consider how you can bring Task 2 more into focus as part of your general meeting structure. This generally contributes to building ecosystems where elephants are not allowed to exist unchallenged for too long.

What Structures Do You Need to Make This Happen?

Establish a structure for your cooperation – and for how you can help each other adhere to this structure!

Remember that the structures and guidelines you establish must always be designed to support your main task.

CHALLENGE 9C: HOW DO I GET STARTED AND MAINTAIN MOMENTUM?

Your efforts may feel like a drop in the ocean, a waste of time that achieves nothing. As when you say, 'Is it just me, or does the atmosphere feel really tense?' and are met with a 'Shhh!' (see Challenge 5). Even if it might feel like a drop in the ocean, it accomplishes the important point of putting a thought or a feeling into words – and making it shared. Problems tend to grow bigger if we do not share them. Psychologists call it rumination when someone is stuck in a cycle of negative thoughts and worries that do not move the person closer to a solution but simply grow increasingly entrenched. The key thing, therefore, is to let some of the air out of the balloon on an ongoing basis – and develop a routine for making this a continual activity.

POINTS FOR REFLECTION

Trust the Process and Measure Progress Inside Your Sphere of Influence

Remember the question we explored in Challenge 5: 'Does it make a difference to stick your neck out if you are met with a "Sshh"?' And remember the conclusion we reached: yes, it does.

It makes a difference if you measure it inside your own sphere of influence: I prodded, I addressed, I spoke up, I pointed out the elephant, I did not simply ignore it … So act where you can (inside your own sphere of influence), and remember to evaluate your efforts within this sphere as well!

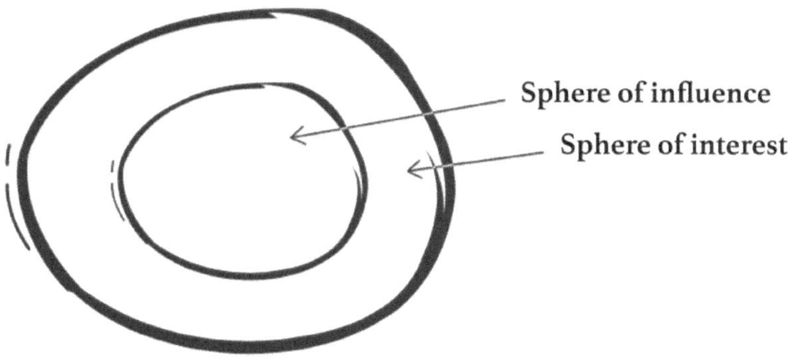

TIPS

Make a Drawing of Your Sphere of Influence

Carry it with you in your mind – and give yourself a pat on the back for everything you do that gradually contributes to preventing elephants from moving about undisturbed.

Write Down All the Micro-Acts That Occur Within Your Own Sphere of Influence

Revisit them often and remind yourself of your contributions.

Consider How You Can Include Your Group in the Process

Maybe you can use the image of your shared sphere of influence to agree on what you will all practise addressing in this context?

MY OWN PAGES

Essential to Me

What gets my attention?

What do I need to pay special attention to?

Micro-Acts I Want to Start With

What (small) step will I take?

When?

With whom?

What difference is it going to make (for me/the group/our mission)?

How will I know that I am succeeding (what will be/feel different in me/in the group/in relation to our mission)?

CHALLENGE 10

DOI: 10.4324/9781003582939-10

Should I let go? Hold on? IS NOW the right time? Or now?

What Is the Right Timing and Dosage When I Want to Bring Up Elephants?

• The Johari Window • The desire to do the right thing • Clear the snow as you go • Create containing • Small things can be addressed as small things • Do not push the snow in front of you

A widely used model in leadership and team development is the Johari Window, which was developed by the psychologists Joseph Luft and Harrington Ingham in 1955. This simple model has remained relevant, as it helps us understand what it might be helpful for us to be mindful of in our communication with others.

The model is often used to examine the so-called open area and to explore whether there are factors in the other areas that might benefit the main task and the group's cooperation if included in the open area: Is there anything in the hidden area that it might be helpful for you to be more open about? And is there anything in the blind spot that others can help you see by offering feedback?

DOI: 10.4324/9781003582939-10

	Known to myself	*Not known to myself*
Known to others	**OPEN AREA** **Information about you that is known to you and others**	**BLIND SPOT** **Information about you that is not known to you but which is known to others**
Not known to others	**HIDDEN AREA** **Information about you that is known only to you**	**UNKNOWN AREA** **Information about you that is not known to you or to others**

Figure 10.1 The Johari Window.

The Johari Window also conveys the important point that it is not everything that should be known to others, but that the open area should match the group's cooperation on the specific main task. Thus, the goal is not simply to expand the open area as much as possible but to expand it where it is meaningful and helpful. This applies both when the hidden area is diminished through greater openness and when the blind spot is diminished through feedback (Figure 10.1).

Many take 'being and acting with authenticity' to mean that the hidden area should be thrown wide open. However, authenticity is not the same as letting it all hang out or allowing others to read you like an open book. Authenticity is being mindful and clear in relation to the open area by asking yourself, 'What might it be important for others to know about me to be able to help, support and challenge me appropriately in relation to our joint main task?'

The same applies to the blind spot: What feedback may it be helpful for us to give each other in order to help, support and challenge each other appropriately in relation to our joint main task?

Now, the question for many people is, 'What is the best way for me to handle it when I notice other people's blind spots?'

WHEN, HOW AND HOW MUCH SHOULD I ADDRESS OTHER PEOPLE'S BLIND SPOTS?

This area is perceived as delicate, which may be precisely why there may be a special wish to 'do the right thing'. To do that, of course, it is important to know exactly what the right thing is. Again, this too depends on the relationship, the context and the main task, but there are a number of factors that may be important to consider.

POINTS FOR REFLECTION

You Can Never Find the Perfect Moment

When an issue feels delicate, it is especially important to consider your own avoidance strategies. You know this from Challenge 4, where you also learnt strategies for providing good feedback. One avoidance strategy related to the question of timing revolves around the desire to find the perfect moment. The desire to say the right thing at exactly the right time can become so compelling that you never find the right moment, meaning that the feedback is delayed or never given.

Give Your Feedback Here and Now – Whenever Possible

As a general rule of thumb, you should provide feedback as close as possible to the experience it relates to.

I often use the image, 'Clear the snow as you go.' Make it a habit to offer continual and immediate feedback on all the good and helpful aspects, as well as the ones that require adjustment and adaptation.

Nothing Is Too Small

Many do not clear the snow as they go because they worry about being seen as a 'nitty gritty type who obsesses over minutiae'. Instead, they make the mistake of waiting until the issues have grown more prominent – perhaps until they have become visible to everyone.

Remember the image of the balloon from Challenge 9: The risk is that it might pop unless you manage continually to let some of the air out.

Create a Containing Environment When the Issue Is Especially Sensitive

And then again ... timing is not completely without significance. Especially in relation to feedback that might seem touchy and therefore should not be provided in passing, or if you notice that the person who is going to receive the feedback is not in a receptive frame of mind.

When an issue is perceived as especially sensitive or when the receiver of the feedback does not appear to be receptive in the moment, set aside some time and create an opportunity for a mindful conversation.

In any case, as always: do not push the snow in front of you.

TIPS

Authorize Yourself

When you are in doubt about dosing your feedback, authorize yourself to take your own experiences seriously. Remember the example with Christian in the open-plan office in Challenge 2.

If a behaviour gets in the way of your work performance or your relationship with a coworker, you should *always* address it. Do not tell yourself it does not mean anything, and do *not* neglect your own experience: Minor issues can be addressed as minor issues. But they should not be ignored.

Practise Clearing the Snow as You Go

Every time you begin to consider when it might be 'the right time', ask yourself, 'Can't I just say it now?' If the answer is 'No', pick a time and a framework – and let the other person know.

MY OWN PAGES

Essential to Me

What gets my attention?

What do I need to pay special attention to?

Micro-Acts I Want to Start With

What (small) step will I take?

When?

____
____
____
____
____

With whom?

____
____
____
____
____

What difference is it going to make (for me/the group/our mission)?

____
____
____
____
____

How will I know that I am succeeding (what will be/feel different in me/in the group/in relation to our mission)?

____
____
____
____
____

Conclusion

When I began the research that forms the basis of *The Elephant in the Room* (2023), a key focus for me was what happens in the moment when working groups neglect Task 2 (our cooperation as a team) and focus exclusively on Task 1 (what we are working together to achieve). What happens in that brief moment when we ignore the 'how', even though it is important for the individual group members, for the group and for the task we are working on?

As part of my research, I took an in-depth look at both at situations in which we succeed in acting on what we notice (incorporating Task 2) and situations in which we do not manage to act on what we notice (avoiding Task 2).

Generally, we tend to avoid looking at Task 2 when we worry about the implications of actively relating to the 'how'. However, this avoidance has consequences. When we ignore Task 3, we also maintain our anxiety, fears or concerns about what would happen if we were to engage.

As captured by the Edgar Schein quotation in the Introduction, the consequence is that we survive by remaining passive. However, that rarely leads to high levels of job satisfaction.

One of the discoveries that stood out in my research was the joy that engagement brings. Not that it is always easy or even necessarily successful, but simply trying carries its own satisfaction. A satisfaction that stems simply from the feeling of taking oneself seriously.

Recently, I worked with a leader who explained, 'I feel taller – and I am going to continue to strive to feel taller in all the contexts I am part of.'

The feeling this leader described is one that I recognize from my own research: When we begin to act on what we notice – rather than retreating – we experience emotions that have to do with feeling more dignified, more valuable and happier. Emotions that are, essentially, associated with the feeling of taking ourselves seriously – standing tall.

It is my hope that you will begin to see the task of dealing with elephants in a new light: Less as an arduous, cumbersome and difficult task and more as a path to engaging fully and believing in yourself and what you find important!

That can be a powerful source of job satisfaction.

References

Adams, M. L. (2015). *Change your questions, change your life.* Berrett Koehler Publishers.

Adler, H., & Sloth, E. (2017). Den svære feedback: Et opgør med hyggehykleriet i feedback-processer fra leder til medarbejder [The difficult feedback: Challenging hypocrisy aimed at avoiding unpleasantness in feedback processes from supervisor to employee]. In A. Trillingsgaard (Ed.), *Feedback gentænkt.* Dansk Psykologisk Forlag.

Argyris, C., & Schön, D. (1974). *Theory in practice: Increasing professional effectiveness.* Jossey-Bass Publishers.

Battilana, J., & Casciaro, T. (2022). *Power, for all: How it really works and why it's everyone's business.* Simon & Schuster.

Binney, G., Wilke, G., & Williams, C. (2005). *Living leadership: A practical guide for ordinary heroes.* Prentice Hall.

Bion, W. (1968). *Experiences in groups and other papers.* Routledge.

Bonnerup, B. (2024). *Et psykodynamisk blik på levende organisationer* [A psychodynamic look at living organizations]. Akademisk Forlag.

Brown, B. (2010, June). *The power of vulnerability* [Video]. TED Conferences. https://www.ted.com/talks/brene_brown_the_power_of_vulnerability

Brown, B. (2012). *Daring greatly: How the courage to be vulnerable transforms the way we live, love, parent and lead.* Penguin.

Brown, B. (2018). *Dare to lead: Brave work, tough conversations, whole hearts.* Random House.

Brunetti, D., & Fincher, D. (2013–2018). *House of cards* [TV series]. Media Rights Capital (MRC); Netflix; Panic Pictures (II); Trigger Street Productions.

Coutu, D. (2002). The anxiety of learning. *Harvard Business Review, 80*(3).
Edmondson, A. (2019). *The fearless organization: Creating psychological safety in the workplace for learning, innovation, and growth*. Wiley.
The Fearless Organization. (n.d.). *Free personal psychological safety survey*. https://fearlessorganizationscan.com/engage/free-personal-psychological-safety-survey
Fogsgaard, M., & Olesen, M. R. (2017). Magtreflekteret feedback [Power-reflected feedback]. In A. Trillingsgaard (Ed.), *Feedback gentænkt*. Dansk Psykologisk Forlag.
Gallo, A. (2017). *HBR guide to dealing with conflict*. Harvard Business Review Press.
Gallo, A. (2023, February 15). What is psychological safety? *Harvard Business Review*. https://hbr.org/2023/02/what-is-psychological-safety
Gervais, M. (2019). How to stop worrying about what other people think of you. *Harvard Business Review*. https://hbr.org/2019/05/how-to-stop-worrying-about-what-other-people-think-of-you
Heffernan, M. (2019, July). *The human skills we need in an unpredictable world* [Video]. TED Conferences. https://www.ted.com/talks/margaret_heffernan_the_human_skills_we_need_in_an_unpredictable_world
Hougaard, R. (2016). *One second ahead: Enhance your performance at work with mindfulness*. Palgrave Macmillan.
Hougaard, R., & Carter, J. (2022). *Compassionate leadership: How to do hard things in a human way*. Harvard Business Review Press.
James, K., & Arroba, T. (2005). Reading and carrying: A framework for learning about emotion and emotionality in organizational systems. *Management Learning, 36*(3), 299–316.
Jungersen, C. (2006). *The exception*. Weidenfeld & Nicolson.
Kahn, W. (2001). Holding environments at work. *The Journal of Applied Behavioral Science, 37*(3), 260–279.
Kegan, R., & Lahey, L. (2009). *Immunity to change: How to overcome it and unlock the potential in yourself and your organization*. Harvard Business Review Press.
Meyerson, D. (2003). *Tempered radicals: How everyday leaders inspire change at work*. Harvard Business School Press.

Meyrowitz, J. (1985). *No sense of place: The impact of electronic media on social behavior.* Oxford University Press.
Ross, R. (1994). Moments of awareness. In P. M. Senge, A. Kleiner, C. Robert, R. B. Ross, & B. J. Smith, *The fifth discipline fieldbook: Strategies and tools for building a learning organization.* Nicholas Brearley Publishing.
Senge, P. M. (1990). *The fifth discipline: The art and practice of the learning organization.* Century Business.
Svalgaard, L. (2015a). *Staying mindful in action: Socioanalytic action research.* SAGE Publications.
Svalgaard, L. (2015b). The struggle of staying with toxic emotions when all you want to do is leave: An exploration of the idea of mindfulness in fostering negative capability. *Socioanalysis, 17,* 43–63.
Svalgaard, L. (2016). Staying mindful in action: The challenge of 'double awareness' on task and process in an action lab. *Action learning: Research and practice, 13*(1), 50–59.
Svalgaard, L. (2017). From real life to real life: Bringing double awareness from action learning programmes into organisational reality. *Action Learning: Research and Practice, 14*(1), 29–49.
Svalgaard, L. (2018). The critical moment of transition: Staying with and acting on newly gained self- and social awareness. *Management Learning, 1*(17), 278–294.
Svalgaard, L. (2023). *The elephant in the room: Engaging with the unsaid in groups and organizations.* Routledge.
Tamm, J. (2004). *Radical collaboration: Five essential skills to overcome defensiveness and build successful relationships.* Harper Business.
Tamm, J. (2015, April). *First step to collaboration: Don't be so defensive!* TED Conferences. https://www.ted.com/talks/jim_tamm_first_step_to_collaboration_don_t_be_so_defensive
Teasdale, J., Williams, M., & Segal, Z. (2013). *The mindful way workbook: An 8-week program to free yourself from depression and emotional distress.* Guilford Press.
Trillingsgaard, A. (2017). Feedback Gentænkt, Dansk Psykologik Forlag, Copenhagen.
Williams, M., Teasdale, J., Segal, Z., & Kabat-Zinn, J. (2008). *The mindful way through depression: Freeing yourself from chronic unhappiness.* Guilford Press.

Notes

1. The solution is shown here.

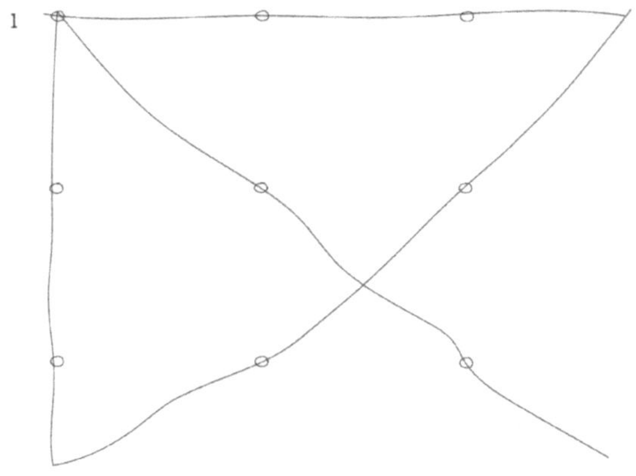

2. Inspired by Amy Edmondson's Personal Psychological Safety Survey (*The Fearless Organization*, 2019).

Index

E

F

G

H

I

J

K

L

Kolibri 360 GmbH
Ferdinand-Jühlke-Straße 7
99095 Erfurt, Deutschland
produktsicherheit@kolibri360.de